KU-777-141

The hands-on guide to post-16 performance and data

Invaluable information for training providers and further education colleges

Nick Linford
Head of the Pearson Research Institute,
Pearson UK, London

LEARNING
RESOURCES
CENTRE

This book is as balanced, practical and accurate as I could make it. Ideas for improvements are always welcome via email to: nick.linford@dataguide.co.uk

For further information and updates visit www.dataguide.co.uk

PEARSON

378.99

A G

138877

Published by Pearson Education Limited, a company incorporated in England and Wales, having its registered office at Edinburgh Gate, Harlow, Essex, CM20 2JE. Registered company number: 872828

Text © Pearson Education Limited, 2010
First published 2010

British Library Cataloguing in Publication Data
A catalogue record for this book is available from the British Library

ISBN 978 1 84690 894 1

All rights reserved. No part of this publication may be reproduced, stored in a retrieval system, or transmitted in any form or by any means, electronic, mechanical, photocopying, recording or otherwise, without the express permission of the Publisher or a licence permitting restricted copying in the United Kingdom issued by the Copyright Licensing Agency Ltd, Saffron House, 6–10 Kirby Street, London EC1 8TS.

To order via the website, go to www.dataguide.co.uk

Illustrations: Nick Linford, London, UK
Publishing consultant: Jenny Penfold
Typesetting and page layout by The Publishing Centre, Oxford, UK
Printed and bound in Great Britain by Ashford Colour Press Ltd., Gosport

Acknowledgements

The publisher would like to thank the following for their permission to reproduce their material:

Extract on p13, How colleges improve, a review of effective practice, Ofsted, September 2008; Extract on p14, Data Quality Framework, the information authority, January 2010; p16, Public Service Delivery Agreement 2, ©Crown copyright 2007; Extract on p18 from Statistical First Release, the data service, December 2009; Extract on p20 from Towards Ambition 2020: skills, jobs, growth, UK Commission for Economic Skills, October 2009; Diagram on p21 from LSC presentation to the information authority board, December 2009; Table on p25 from ILR Specification, LSC, 2010; Extract on p29 from ILR Specification 09/10 and 10/11, the information authority; Diagram on p35 from Qualification Journey – Accreditation to Publication on LAD, the Data Service, December 2009; Extracts on p60 and p61 from Identifying and Managing Underperformance, LSC, December 2009; Extracts on p64 and p67 from VA and DT for 16–18 learners: LAT Handbook 2007/08, LSC, 2008; Extract on p70 from DCSF website, Post-16 contextual value added 2008 model, DCSF; Extract on p73 from the Framework for Excellence website, LSC, December 2009; Extracts on p80, from Framework for Excellence website: Improvements made for 2009/10 as a result of implementation in 2008/09, LSC, November 2009; An Introductory Guide for College Governors, LSC, May 2009; Launch Press release, June 2008; Extracts on p80 and p81from Skills for Growth, the national skills strategy, Department for Business, Innovation and Skills, © Crown Copyright, 2009; Table on p83 modelled on the Data Quality Framework, the information authority, January 2010; Extract on p88 from How colleges improve, a review of effective practice, Ofsted, September 2008; Extract on p90 from Funding Guidance, 2008/9, LSC; Extract on p90 from DSAT v.10.00 User Guide, LSC, December 2009; Extracts on p93, p95, p98 from Handbook for the inspection of FE and skills, Ofsted, 2010; Extract on p95 from Common inspection framework for FE and skills, Ofsted, 2009; Extracts on p99, p100 and p10 from How colleges improve, a review of effective practice, Ofsted, 2008; Graph on p100 from Talisman Issue 80, Ofsted, December 2009.

The publisher would like to thank the following for their kind permission to reproduce their photographs:

(Key: b-bottom; c-centre; l-left; r-right; t-top)

Cover images: *Front:* **iStockphoto:** br, Magdalena Jankowska tr, Andreas Reh cr; **Photolibrary.com:** Rodolfo Benitez / age fotostock c; *Back:* **iStockphoto:** cl; **Photolibrary.com:** Goodshoot bl, Joff Lee / Fresh Food Images tl

All other images © Pearson Education

Every effort has been made to trace copyright holders and we apologise in advance for any unintentional omissions. We would be pleased to insert the appropriate acknowledgement in any subsequent edition of this publication.

The websites quoted in this book were correct and up to date at the time of publication.

Content overview

Glossary of abbreviations 6

Introduction and Comments from across the sector 9

The context 12

The Individualised Learner Record (ILR) 22

The Learning Aim Database (LAD) 32

The Learner Information Suite (LIS) 42

Success rates and MLPs 52

Learner progress 62

Framework for Excellence (FfE) 72

Data quality 82

Inspection and self-assessment 92

Agencies and organisations 102

Performance and data calendar 112

Notes 128

Detailed Contents

Glossary of abbreviations	6
Author's introduction	9
Comments from across the sector	10

The context — 12
The importance of post-16 performance and data	14
Targets, priorities and national indicators	16
Statistical First Releases	18
The future of post-16 performance and data	20

The Individualised Learner Record (ILR) — 22
The ILR specification	24
ILR field numbers and names	26
ILR returns	28
ILR changes for 2010/11	30

The Learning Aim Database — 32
From accreditation to the Learning Aim Database	34
The Learning Aim Database online	36
Learning aims	38
Other online qualification search engines	40

The Learner Information Suite (LIS) — 42
Preparing the LIS for use	44
The LIS and learner-responsive provision	46
The LIS and employer-responsive provision	48
Advanced use of the LIS	50

Success rates and MLPs — 52
Learner-responsive success rates	54
Employer-responsive success rates	56
Minimum Levels of Performance (MLP)	58
Identifying and managing underperformance	60

Learner progress — 62
Value Added overview	64
The Learner Achievement Tracker	66
Value Added reports	68
Contextualised Value Added	70

Framework for Excellence (FfE)　　72
　Framework for Excellence overview　　74
　The core FfE performance indicators　　76
　The specific FfE performance indicators　　78
　Using the Framework for Excellence　　80

Data quality　　82
　Data accuracy, validity and good practice　　84
　Data credibility and quality assessment reports　　86
　Success rate data credibility　　88
　Data audit and comparison tools　　90

Inspection and self-assessment　　92
　Ofsted inspection overview　　94
　Full inspection reports and grades　　96
　Self-assessment reports　　98
　Improving self-assessment　　100

Agencies and organisations　　102
　The Data Service　　104
　The information authority　　106
　Managing Information Across Partners　　108
　Other performance and data related organisations　　110

　Performance and data calendar　　112
　Notes　　128

Glossary of abbreviations

AAT: Achievement and Attainment Tables

ACL: Adult Community Learning

ADaM: Achievement and Data Management software

ALAC: Adult Learner Account Calculator

ALIS: Advanced Level Information System

ALN: Additional learning needs

ALP: Association of Learning Providers

ALPS: Advanced Level Performance System

ALR: Adult learner-responsive

ALS: Additional Learning Support

AMPS: Allocations Management and Payments System

AO: Awarding organisation

AoC: Association of Colleges

ASL: Adult safeguarded learning

ASN: Additional social needs

BIS: Department for Business Innovation and Skills

CAA: Common Area Assessment

CIF: Common inspection framework

CIS: College information systems

CSR: Comprehensive Spending Review

CVA: Contextualised Value Added

DCSF: Department for Children Schools and Families

DLC: Demand Led Calculator

DLF: Demand-led funding

DSAT: Data Self-Assessment Toolkit

DV: Derived Variable

E2E: Entry to Employment

EDRS: Employer Data Registration Service

EDS: Employer Data Service

ER: employer-responsive

ESF: European Social Fund

ESF SR: European Social Fund Short Record

ESOL: English for speakers of other languages

FE: Further education

FfE: Framework for Excellence

FL: Foundation Learning

FLLN: Family Literacy, Language and Numeracy

FMCE: Financial Management and Control Evaluation

FTE: Full Time Equivalent

GLH: Guided learning hour

GQ: General qualification

HE: Higher education

HEFCE: Higher Education Funding Council for England

HEIFES: Higher Education in Further Education: Students Survey

HESA: Higher Education Statistics Agency

HMCI: Her Majesties Chief Inspectorate

IA: Information authority

IAG: Information, Advice and Guidance

IAL: Informal Adult Learning

ILP: Individual Learning Plan

ILR: Individualised Learner Record

IMUP: Indentifying and managing underperformance

JACQA: Joint Advisory Committee for Qualifications Approval

JISC: Joint Information Systems Committee

KPI: Key performance indicator

LA: Local Authority

LAA: Local area agreement

LAD: Learning Aim Database

LAMS: Learner Accounts Management System

LAT: Learner Achievement Tracker

LDCS: Learning Directory Classification System

LIS: Learner Information Suite

LR: learner-responsive

LRS: Learner Registration Service

LSC: Learning and Skills Council

LSF: Learner Support Fund

LSIS: Learning and Skills Improvement Service

MIAP: Managing Information Across Partners

MIS: Management information systems

MLP: Minimum Levels of Performance

NAS: National Apprenticeship Service

NCF: National Commissioning Framework

NDAQ: National Database of Accredited Qualifications

NEET: Not in education, training or employment

NES: National Employer Service

NI: National Indicator

NILTA: National Information and Learning Technology Alliance

NLDC: Neighbourhood Learning in Deprived Communities

NQF: National Qualification Framework

NTI: Notice To Improve

NVQ: National Vocational Qualification

Ofqual: Office of the Qualifications and Examinations Regulator

Ofsted: Office for Standards in Education, Children's Services and Skills

OLASS: Offender Learning and Skills Service

OLDC: Online Data Collections

PaMS: Planning and Modelling System

PCDL: Personal and Community Development Learning

PFR: Provider Funding Report

PI: Performance indicator

PIMS: Provider Information Management System

PLA: Programme led Apprenticeship

PLP: Personalised Learning Programmes

PLRS: Personal Learning Record Service

POL: Provider online

PSA: Public Service Agreement

PVS: Planning Volumes Sheet

QAN: Qualification Accreditation Number

QCA: Qualifications and Curriculum Authority

QCDA: Qualifications and Curriculum Development Agency

QCF: Qualifications and Credit Framework

QSR: Qualification Success Rate

RAG: Red, amber and green

RMF: Record of Main Findings

SAMS: Single Account Management System

SAR: Self-assessment report

SFA: Skills Funding Agency

SFC: Sector framework code

SFL: Skills for Life

SFR: Statistical First Release

SLN: Standard learner number

SOC: Standard Occupational Classification

SRP: Strategic Reporting Platform

SSA: Sector subject area

SSB: Standard Setting Bodies

SSC: Sector Skills Council

SSoA: Summary Statement of Activity

TQS: Training Quality Standard

TtG: Train to Gain

Ufl: University for Industry

UKCES: UK Commission for Employment and Skills

UKPRN: UK Provider Reference Number

UKRLP: UK Register of Learning Providers

UKVQRP: UK Vocational Qualification Reform Programme

ULN: Unique Learning Number

UPIN: Unique Provider Identification Number

VA: Value added

VQ: Vocational qualification

WBL: Work Based Learning

WFL: Wider Family Learning

YPLA: Young People's Learning Agency

Note

To assist the reader a number of web addresses have been included within this book. These include addresses to locations on the Learning and Skills Council website, which as an agency ceased to exist from April 2010. Therefore, in the absence of new addresses at the time of writing, it is hoped that users will automatically be redirected.

Author's introduction

The hands-on guide to post-16 performance and data has been written as a reference guide for all staff working within the post-16 education and training sector. It covers topics such as why data is important, what data is collected, and how it is interpreted for the purposes of performance management and inspection. However, this guide cannot be the authoritative source of information on data and performance, as that remains with the Young People's Learning Agency, the Skills Funding Agency, and Ofsted.

Following the success of *The hands-on guide to post-16 funding* (www.fundingguide.co.uk) we decided to write a complementary title that reflects the importance of data in post-16 education. Too little comprehensive guidance exists about this critical topic, at a time when self-regulation and improvement are being encouraged. As the public purse tightens, the relative performance of colleges and training providers is becoming more important than ever to the commissioning agencies.

This hands-on guide, like the funding version, contains ten chapters, and the topics covered within each are spread across two pages. This serves two purposes. Firstly, it makes it easier for you to find information without the need for an index. Secondly, having two pages per topic ensures that only the main and most important points have been included.

This book is also designed to appeal to a wide range of staff. It contains many diagrams, screen-shot images, tables and worked examples to help bring to life a potentially impenetrable subject. It should also appeal to the teachers and trainers who will be contributing to self-assessment reports and quality improvement action plans.

I have had invaluable assistance of an editorial board consisting of key staff within a number of the relevant agencies: the Learning and Skills Council, the Data Service, *the information authority*, and Ofsted. I would therefore like to thank Darren Bassett, Lisa McDougall, Anne Fessi, Fazia Saleem, David Young, Chris Lewis, Ellie Fraizer, Sue Parker and Mike Davis for their support, comments and suggestions.

In particular, I would like to thank Darren Bassett, formerly of the Data Service and now at the Young People's Learning Agency. He is a true professional who saw the benefits of producing this guide and arranged for a financial contribution to its production. Thanks also to those technically involved in the publishing of this book, including Jenny Penfold, Stephen Ashton and Joanne Allcock.

Much of the writing took place during the 2009 Christmas break, so I reserve the final thanks, and apologies, for my beautiful wife Sarah.

Comments from across the sector

The post-16 system in England is supported by a wealth of data sources, such as the Individualised Learner Record, which provides more complete and timely data on further education than any other country in Europe. The importance of data is higher today than it has ever been before, and this book highlights many best practice techniques for providers to manage data and performance. I expect this to become a key tool for not only providers, but also for other data users in the sector as we work together to drive improvements in the quality of data that are collected and used for the benefit of the sector.

Rich Williams, Head of the Data Service

This guide aims to support providers in their understanding of data and performance and will serve as a valuable tool in the collection and management of learner data. I'm pleased to see that it contains some good advice on how to develop best practice and comply with current requirements for reporting data to the standards and validation rules set by *the information authority*.

John Perks, Head of *the information authority*

At Lewisham College we operate a culture of performance management which is dedicated to driving up standards and the quality of everything we do. In particular, our annual curriculum planning and performance cycle involves staff and learners throughout the college, all of whom interpret data to inform decisions and evidence change. This guide to performance and data is an invaluable reference tool which everyone involved in the delivery of post-16 education and training should have close to hand.

Maxine Room, Principal of Lewisham College

The Learning and Skills Improvement Service is supporting colleges and training providers to raise standards in the context of self-improvement. In particular, the collection and use of high quality data is a prerequisite for honest self-assessment and the monitoring of quality improvement plans. What makes this guide so invaluable is that it will really help teachers and trainers understand how the qualities of their courses are judged by the commissioning and inspection agencies.

David Collins, Chief Executive of the Learning and Skills Improvement Service (LSIS)

Further Education Colleges are complex and sophisticated organisations that collect a vast amount of data about their learners and the programmes that they study. For this data to return any value it needs to be of high quality, and for this reason colleges invest significant resources ensuring it is complete and valid. It is then used by staff and learners throughout the college to set and monitor a broad range of challenging but achievable targets which support and evidence continuous self-improvement. This hands-on guide is an excellent resource for everyone with an interest in the performance of both learners and colleges.

Martin Doel, Chief Executive of the Association of Colleges (AoC)

Against a backdrop of public sector cuts it has never been more important for learning providers to demonstrate that they can meet targets and deliver ever higher quality training opportunities. It is also important to our members that they use the data they collect to monitor their own performance, and implement improvement plans accordingly. This book is an excellent introduction to data and performance frameworks within post-16 education. It is essential reading for everyone from the trainer to the Managing Director.

Graham Hoyle, Chief Executive of the Association of Learning Providers (ALP)

The context

> A successful college or training provider can not survive without a detailed understanding of the relationship between student performance, government targets, funding and cost control.
>
> Neil Reed, Senior Associate Director, MCA Cooper Associates

The importance of post-16 performance and data

Targets, priorities and national indicators

Statistical First Releases

The future of post-16 performance and data

Performance and data in the post-16 education and training sector is collected and reported in a variety of ways, and at different times of the year. This book primarily describes performance and data regimes within the demand-led funding models of learner- and employer-responsive provision. Before funding methodology reforms in 2008/09 this provision would have been referred to as further education (FE) and work-based learning (WBL).

Post-16 education and training referred to in this book

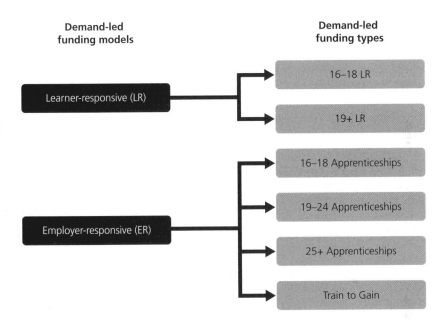

The Department for Children, Schools and Families (DCSF) funds provision for those under the age of 19, and the Department for Business Innovation and Skills (BIS) funds those aged 19 and over. A number of new agencies, such as the Young People's Learning Agency (YPLA) and the Skills Funding Agency, distribute the funding to providers (via the local authorities for those aged under 19). They also develop, manage and administer data, performance and the commissioning regime.

As you read this book, it is important to remember that performance and data is important and useful to all staff, not least those that actually teach and train learners. "Getting the data right and getting staff to take ownership of data and be accountable for them is critical. All teachers and curriculum managers have to understand the data, why they are needed and how to use them. Then analysing and interpreting data becomes an essential tool, enabling staff to be self-critical and accurate in their self-assessment and in measuring progress and improvement." (*How colleges improve, a review of effective practice*, Ofsted, September 2008)

13

The importance of post-16 performance and data

Every time a learner enrols on a course a significant amount of data needs to be collected and updated, which is important to a variety of users.

Importance to government departments and agencies
- Set strategic direction and stretching targets.
- Measure international competitiveness and efficiencies.
- Monitor the system, providers and measure performance.
- Identify gaps and issues that inform policy development.
- Evidence for commissioning and decommissioning provision.
- Help providers deliver the policies and priorities.
- Help people make choices about what learning to undertake.

Importance to providers
- Income is based on data returned to funding bodies.
- Performance will influence access to public funding.
- Identify gaps and issues that inform strategic development.
- Challenging and achievable targets set and monitored to improve key improvement indicators, such as quality and value for money.

Importance of data quality
As data plays a significant role in the post-16 education sector, the quality of the data is particularly important. Providers invest a significant level of resource to ensure their data is accurate, valid, complete, consistent and timely (*p.83*). This paragraph from *the information authority* Data Quality Framework highlights the benefits and costs of variable data quality.

> Good quality data leads to accurate success rates, correct funding and the ability to track progress accurately against key performance measures and government targets. Poor quality data leads to inconsistencies in funding, planning and strategic decision-making. The potential consequences of poor quality data could range from the unequal distribution of learning opportunities across the country to individual learners being denied the access to the correct level of funding for training opportunities. This is not the desirable outcome either for Learners, the FE Sector, Local or Central Government or ultimately the Taxpayer.
>
> Source: *Data Quality Framework*, the information authority (January 2010)

Data returns, software and reporting
The majority of data referred to in this book derives from provider student systems in the form of an Individualised Learner Record (*p.22*). The flow diagram on the following page shows how this nationally specified data is used for funding and other performance-related purposes.

Data and performance information flow diagram

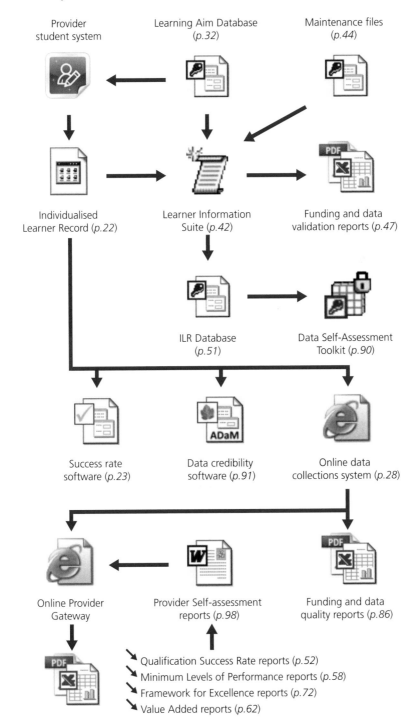

Provider student system

Learning Aim Database (p.32)

Maintenance files (p.44)

Individualised Learner Record (p.22)

Learner Information Suite (p.42)

Funding and data validation reports (p.47)

ILR Database (p.51)

Data Self-Assessment Toolkit (p.90)

Success rate software (p.23)

Data credibility software (p.91)

Online data collections system (p.28)

Online Provider Gateway

Provider Self-assessment reports (p.98)

Funding and data quality reports (p.86)

Qualification Success Rate reports (p.52)
Minimum Levels of Performance reports (p.58)
Framework for Excellence reports (p.72)
Value Added reports (p.62)

Targets, priorities and national indicators

The government prioritise the use of public funding by setting and measuring contributions to national targets and priorities.

Public Service Agreement targets

The most significant targets, arguably for every part of the public sector, are the Public Service Agreement (PSA) targets. This is because PSA targets are set by the government's Treasury Department. They underpin the budgets received by each government department as part of the Comprehensive Spending Review (CSR). Therefore DCSF and BIS spending are being judged against their ability to achieve their PSA targets, so they heavily influence their policies and how they prioritise the funding they pass on to providers accordingly. The tables below outline two of a number of PSA targets that are the responsibility of BIS to achieve.

PSA target 2.1
Proportion of people of working age achieving functional literacy and numeracy skills
Target
597,000 people of working age (aged 16–64 inclusive) to achieve a first Level 1 or above literacy qualification, and 390,000 to achieve a first entry Level 3 or above numeracy qualification
Baseline
0 at start of 2008/09, measured until end of 2010/11
Data source
Individualised Learner Record (ILR). Supported by Skills for Life survey
Frequency of reporting
Annually in the Statistical First Release

PSA target 2.2
Proportion of working-age adults qualified to at least full Level 2
Target
79 per cent of working-age adults (men aged 19–64 and women aged 19–59) qualified to at least full Level 2
Baseline
This equates with 1,217,000 publicly funded achievements between 2008 and 2011
Data Source
Labour Force Survey/Integrated Household Survey
Frequency of reporting
Annually in the Statistical First Release

http://www.hm-treasury.gov.uk/d/pbr_csr07_psa2.pdf

Summary Statement of Activity

In recent years providers have been required to submit Summary Statements of Activity (SSoA), which include information about the volume of learners and the target-bearing provision that they will be undertaking. This helps the relevant funding agency commission providers that can contribute to PSA and targets as described within investment strategies. Provision which does not contribute to these targets is labelled as non-priority or developmental learning.

National Indicators (NI) for local authorities

As part of the 2007–2010 CSR the Government introduced a new single set of 198 national indicators for English local authorities and local authority partnerships. A list of these indicators, which flow from the priorities identified in PSA targets, can be found at http://tinyurl.com/ys5nww

> The outcomes they measure and the indicators themselves provide a clear statement of Government's priorities for delivery by local government and its partners over the next three years. They will be the only indicators on which central government will be able to set targets for local government.
>
> Source: *National Indicators for Local Authorities: Handbook of Definitions*, DCLG, 2007

National Indicators will become increasingly important for providers because in April 2010 local authorities became responsible for funding all learner- and employer-responsive provision for those aged under 19. For example, the National Indicators referred to in the DCSF *16–19 Statement of Priorities and Investment Strategy for 2010/11* were:

NI19 Rate of proven re-offending by young offenders

NI45 Young offenders' engagement in suitable education, employment or training

NI79 Achievement of a Level 2 qualification by the age of 19

NI80 Achievement of a Level 3 qualification by the age of 19

NI81 Inequality gap in the achievement of a Level 3 qualification by the age of 19

NI82 Inequality gap in the achievement of a Level 2 qualification by the age of 19

NI90 Take up of 14–19 learning diplomas

NI91 Participation of 17-year-olds in education or training

NI117 16–18-year-olds who are not in education, training or employment (NEET)

NI148 Care leavers in employment, education or training

Local authorities will also increasingly be involved in the planning of English for Speakers of Other Languages (ESOL) provision.

NI13 Migrants' English language skills and knowledge

Statistical First Releases

Statistical First Releases

One of the main sources of statistical information for further education is the Statistical First Release (SFR) on Post-16 Education. This is a quarterly publication produced by the Data Service on behalf of the Department for Business, Innovation and Skills (BIS) in consultation with BIS and the Department for Children, Schools and Families (DCSF) statisticians. Information from the different post-16 learning options is drawn together to give a comprehensive picture of the participation and attainment of young people and adults (primarily those funded as learner- and employer-responsive).

The SFR is published in PDF format alongside the following data. It is broken down by Government Office Region and Local Authority:

- Further education and skills participation by level and age
- Further education and skills achievement by level and age
- Further education success rates by age
- Apprenticeships starts by level
- Apprenticeship framework completions
- Train to Gain starts by level
- Train to Gain achievements by level
- Train to Gain success rates.

The SFR can be downloaded alongside the Excel tables containing the data from www.thedataservice.org.uk/statistics

The SFR is published in:
- March, which includes updated participation and achievement data;
- June, which includes in-year participation and mid-year estimates;
- October, which includes a first view of full-year participation;
- December, which includes a provisional view of participation and achievement for learner-responsive provision, as well as final information for apprenticeships and Train to Gain.

Alongside the SFR tables, the supporting data includes breakdowns by age, gender, ethnicity, learners with learning difficulties and/or disabilities and/or health problems, region, local authority, parliamentary constituency, sector and funding stream. The Data Service also published quarter one apprenticeship and Train to Gain starts and achievements for 2009/10 (Annex A to the SFR). However, caution is advised as the Data Service forecasts that the figures in Annex A could rise by as much as 40% once providers have included all the data in their returns (p.28).

The March 2010 edition of the SFR includes:

- final 2008/09 data for learner- and employer-responsive provision;
- 2009 information from the Labour Force Survey, showing the level of highest qualification held for both working age and economically active sub-groups of the population;
- estimates of the number of vocational qualifications awarded in the UK in 2009;
- success rate Information for 2008/09 for FE colleges and providers;
- information on Apprenticeship and Train to Gain starts and achievements for the first six months of the 2009/10 academic year;
- information on Learner Responsive (including Further Education, Adult Community Learning and University for Industry) participation for the first three months of the 2009/10 academic year.

Note
As a consequence of the new demand-led funding methodology, figures from 2008/09 are not directly comparable with those for earlier years (with the exception of Apprenticeship and Train to Gain starts). This is explained in more detail via this link: http://tinyurl.com/yfcr9k6

Additional research and statistics
The DCSF and BIS manage a research and statistics gateway via their website (www.dcsf.gov.uk/rsgateway), in which SFRs are announced alongside other education-related research and statistics (particularly for schools and HE). Other statistics produced by the DCSF include, for example, the number of learners enrolled as at September 2009 on 14–19 diploma programmes, by local authority, level and sector: http://tinyurl.com/yezkqjo

Other organisations producing education statistics include:
- Economic and Social Data Service (for the Labour Force Survey)
  www.esds.ac.uk

- Higher Education Statistics Agency
  www.hesa.ac.uk

- Joint Council for Qualifications
  www.jcq.org.uk

- National Audit Office
  www.nao.org.uk

- Office for National Statistics
  www.statistics.gov.uk

- UK Commission for Employment and Skills
  www.ukces.org.uk

The future of post-16 performance and data

Every year there are changes to post-16 data requirements and performance information. However, it is expected that the next few months will involve more change than usual. This is being driven by the creation of two separate funding bodies (the YPLA and Skills Funding Agency), and a desire to create greater transparency and accountability. These two pages take a closer look at just a few of the significant changes being considered at present.

Framework for Excellence (FfE)

The FfE is the 'unified post-16 performance assessment' which was first nationally piloted in 2008/09 (*p. 72*). It is expected that scores will be published on a dedicated website in June 2010 and that schools will also begin to be judged using FfE performance indicators. The FfE is likely to continue to be reformed, which might, for example, include the addition of an educational inclusion indicator to recognise those providers that are most successful at narrowing attainment gaps.

More significant changes have been promoted by the UK Commission for Economic Skills (UKCES), which have been welcomed by the government. The box below includes some of their initial thinking (also see page 81).

A new and public institutional performance framework for learning providers, a balanced scorecard, based on their profile of aggregate outcomes/destinations, customer satisfaction levels, and quality, balanced against evidence of the economic, social and labour market characteristics of their local catchment area (see below).

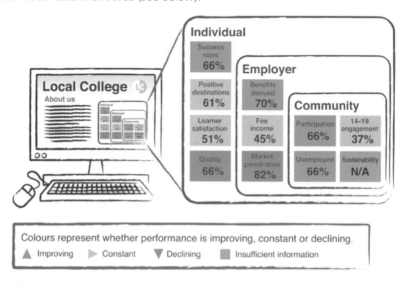

Source: *Towards Ambition 2020: skills, jobs, growth*, UKCES (October 2009)

Changes to the Individualised Learner Record (ILR)

The ILR is the nationally specified data returned by providers (*p.22*). Every year *the information authority* manages a change process, which involves consulting the sector. Anyone can submit a Request for Change form before Friday 18 June 2010, which will then be reviewed by a stakeholder panel before going out to consultation. *The information authority* board will then decide which changes will be implemented for 2011/12, as described on page 106. ILR changes will also be informed by a new 'learner data strategy', which was commissioned in November 2009 by *the information authority*.

The Single Account Management System (SAMS)

The Skills Funding Agency have been developing an online 'settlement system' to support providers and Skills Funding Agency staff with single contract negotiations, provider payments, performance monitoring, triggering intervention and the reallocation of funding where required. SAMS is being developed in a series of stages until 2013, and will include reports and dashboard views.

How the Single Account Management System might look

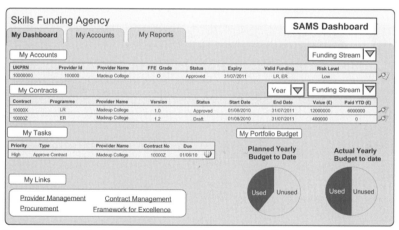

Source: *LSC presentation* to the information authority board (02/12/09)

Programme and credit success rates

Perhaps the most well known performance measures in post-16 education and training are success rates. Recently, changes were made to the calculation method for qualification success rates (*p.52*). However, the YPLA and Skills Funding Agency are also piloting the use of programme and credit success rate measures. For example, a learner who achieves three of their four qualifications within a 14–19 Diploma would have a qualification success rate of 75%, but a programme success rate of 0%. Equally, a learner who achieves three out of four credits would have a 75% credit success rate but a 0% qualification success rate. Further information about these new methodologies will be announced on The Data Service website (*p.104*).

The Individualised Learner Record

> The ILR is at the heart of the whole set of data needed to effectively analyse performance. If this is understood and it is fed and maintained effectively the rest should follow. Get it wrong and you have problems!
>
> Mark Hill, Vice Principal Curriculum and Quality, Lambeth College

The ILR specification

ILR field numbers and names

ILR returns

ILR changes for 2010/11

The Individualised Learner Record (ILR) is used for both learner- and employer-responsive provision to collect data about the learners and the learning that they undertake. The ILR specification is produced by *the information authority*, which is available from their website (*p.105*).

The ILR Structure
The ILR consists of data set fields for learners, learning aims and HE.

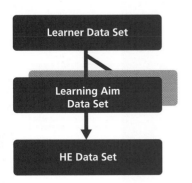

All learners will have a single learner data set. These are ILR L fields (*p.26*)

A learner will have a learning aim data set for each enrolment (including programme aims). These are ILR A fields (*p.26*)

A Higher Education (HE) data set is required for every Level 4, Level 5 or HE enrolment. These are ILR H fields (*p.27*)

ILR returns
ILR files are returned online, the deadlines for which are published by *the information authority* in Appendix H of the ILR specification (*p.24*).

ILR cycle of returns	Frequency (*p.29*)
Learner-responsive	Five returns for the year
Employer-responsive	Monthly in line with the timetable

Software can also import ILR files to, for example, generate funding and data validation reports or calculate retention, achievement and success rates or compare the data between two different ILR files.

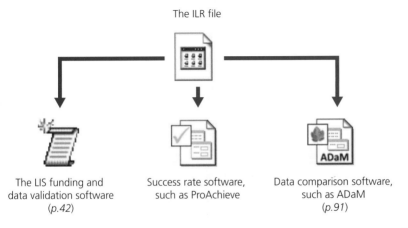

The ILR file

The LIS funding and data validation software (*p.42*)

Success rate software, such as ProAchieve

Data comparison software, such as ADaM (*p.91*)

The ILR specification

The most up-to-date version of the technical specification for the ILR is available to download from *the information authority* website (*p.105*), and it is commonly referred to as the ILR specification. The specification for the relevant academic year includes the ILR structure, data fields and valid entries.

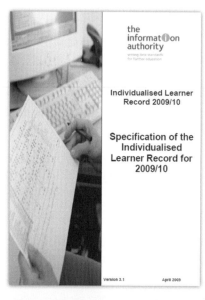

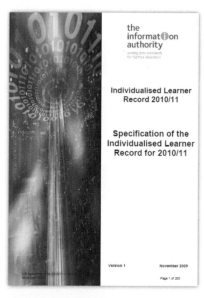

Specification of the ILR for 2009/10 (v3.1)	205 pages
Additional appendixes to ILR specification	
A Collections timetable	8 pages
B Migration information	17 pages
C Valid postcode format	2 pages
D Country of domicile codes	9 pages
E Local LSC numbers	1 page
F Data protection statement	1 page
G Prior attainment levels	2 pages
H Learning aim class codes	23 pages
I Forms and forms guidance	1 page
L Summary of SOC 2000 codes	6 pages
N Special projects and pilot codes	29 pages
O National learning aim monitoring codes	12 pages
P Data quality, standards and field ownership	19 pages

In addition to the ILR specification, numerous guidance and validation rule documents, ILR presentations, ILR forms and provider support manuals can be downloaded from *the information authority* website.

Example ILR data field

The table below shows the valid entries for the prior attainment field. If valid codes are not used the Learner Information Suite (LIS) would apply a validation rule (L35_1) and highlight the error (*p.84*).

Field	L35	Prior attainment level		
Required for	LR and ER	**Field length**	2	**Field type**	Numeric
Description	The learner's prior attainment when they first enrol with the provider.			
Reason required	To allow analysis of the level of prior attainment of learners, to help with value-added analyses and to ensure funding and delivery is targeted at key groups.			
Valid entries	09	Entry level		
	07	Other qualifications below Level 1		
	01	Level 1		
	02	Full Level 2		
	03	Full Level 3		
	04	Level 4		
	05	Level 5 and above		
	97	Other qualification, level not known		
	98	Not known		
	99	No qualifications		

Source: *ILR Specification 2010/11* (v.1)

The ILR specification document also contains any related notes and validation rules for the relevant data field.

The prior attainment ILR field is particularly important to the government as it is used to help determine whether learners have the potential to contribute to public service agreement (PSA) targets (*p.16*). Providers should therefore be aware that:

- the use of level not known (code 97) and not known (code 98) should not be used if the learning aim is a full Level 2 or full Level 3 (*p.87*);
- prior attainment is the subject of credibility checks (*p.86*);
- there is a good practice guide by PWC here: http://tinyurl.com/ykqajka
- there is a good practice guide by RCU here: http://tinyurl.com/ybefmsf
- there is a Skills Strategy explanation here: http://tinyurl.com/ydf8zc7
- Appendix G of the ILR Specification should be consulted to determine a learner's prior attainment;
- and there is also a website to assist: www.qualificationscalculator.co.uk

ILR field numbers and names

These two pages are designed to be a handy list of all the ILR field names and numbers. However, the latest ILR specification is the definitive source of information (*p.24*). Note: some fields occur more than once.

No.	Learner field name
L01	Provider Number
L02	Contract/Allocation type♠●
L03	Learner reference number
L04	Data set identifier
L05	Learning aim data sets
L07	HE data sets
L08	Deletion flag♦
L09	Learner surname
L10	Learner forename
L11	Date of birth
L12	Ethnicity
L13	Sex
L14	Learning difficulties
L15	Disability
L16	Learning difficulty
L17	Home postcode
L18	Address line 1
L19	Address line 2
L20	Address line 3
L21	Address line 4
L22	Current postcode
L23	Telephone number
L24	Country of domicile
L25	Number of funding LSC♣
L26	NI number
L27	Restricted use indicator
L28	Eligibility for enhanced funding
L29	Additional learning support♠
L31	Additional learning support cost♠
L32	Eligibility for disadvantage uplift♠
L33	Disadvantage uplift factor♠
L34	Learner support reason
L35	Prior attainment level
L36	Learner status on last day before working♦
L37	Employment status on first day of learning
L39	Destination

No.	Learner field name cont.
L40	National learner monitoring
L41	Local learner monitoring
L42	Provider-specified learner data
L44	NES delivery LSC number♦♣
L45	Unique learner number
L46	UK provider reference number
L47	Current employment status♦
L48	Date employment status changed♦
L49	Discretionary support funds♠

No.	Aim field name
A01	Provider number
A02	Contract/Allocation type
A03	Learner reference number
A04	Data set identifier
A05	Learning aim data set sequence
A07	HE data sets
A08	Data set format
A09	Learning aim reference
A10	Funding stream/model
A11	Source of funding
A13	Tuition fee received for year♠
A14	Reason for full funding/co-funding of learning aim
A15	Programme type
A16	Programme entry route♦
A17	Delivery mode♠
A18	Main delivery mode
A19	Employer role♠
A20	Re-take♠
A21	Franchised-out and partnership arrangement♣
A22	Franchise and partnership delivery provider number
A23	Delivery location postcode
A26	Framework code
A27	Learning start date
A28	Learning planned end date
A31	Learning actual end date
A32	Guided learning hours♠

No.	Aim field name cont.
A34	Completion status
A35	Learning outcome
A36	Learning outcome grade
A40	Achievement date♦
A44	Employer identifier
A45	Workplace location postcode
A46	National learning aim monitoring
A47	Local learning aim monitoring
A48	Provider specified learning aim data
A49	Special projects and pilots
A50	Reason learning ended
A51a	Proportion of funding remaining
A52	Distance learning SLN♠
A53	Additional learning needs♦
A54	Broker contract number♣
A55	Unique learner number
A56	UK provider reference number
A57	Source of tuition fees♠
A58	ASL provision type♠
A59	Planned credit value
A60	Credits achieved
A61	Project dossier number
A62	ESF local project number
A63	National Skills Academy
A64	Planned group-based hours♦
A65	Planned one-to-one contact hours♦
A66	Employment status on day before starting learning aim
A67	Length of unemployment before starting ESF project
A68	Employment outcome
A69	Eligibility for enhanced funding♥♦
A70	Contracting organisation code♥

No.	HE field name (LR only)
H01	Provider number
H02	Contract/Allocation type●
H03	Learner reference number
H04	Data set identifier code
H05	Learning aim data set sequence
H07	HE data set sequence
H09	Student instance identifier
H10	Nationality
H11	Highest qualification on entry
H12	New entrant to HE
H13	Type of instance year
H14	Mode of study
H15	Level applicable to Funding Council HESES
H16	Completion of year instance
H20	Major source of tuition fees
H21	Term-time accommodation
H23	Occupation code
H24	Last institution attended
H31	Reason for ending instance
H34	Percentage taught in third LDCS subject
H35	Percentage taught in third LDCS subject
H36	Socio-economic indicator
H37	Unique learner number
H38	UK provider reference number
H39	UCAS tariff points
H40	UCAS personal identifier
H41	UCAS application code
H42	Special fee indicator
H43	Learner FTE completed
H44	NHS Bursary
H45	Qualification on entry♥

Key:

♠ Learner-responsive returns only

♦ Employer-responsive returns only

♥ New for 2010/11

♣ Removed for 2010/11

● Blank fields for 2010/11

See page 30

ILR returns

Both learner- and employer-responsive ILR files are returned by providers who upload it to the Data Service's online data collections (OLDC) system.

Screen-shot of the OLDC

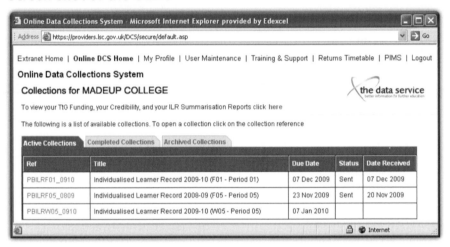

Some providers, usually with relatively few learners, return ILR data directly, record by record, using the provider online (POL) system.

> **Note**
>
> It is strongly recommended that providers use the Learner Information Suite (LIS) software to validate the ILR before returning data (*p.42*). In addition, many providers will run their own data credibility reports and use the Data Self-Assessment Toolkit (DSAT) prior to returning ILR data (*p.86*).

The LR ILR files change from being named F files in 2009/10 to LR files in 2010/11. Monthly ER ILR files also change names, from W files to ER files.

Once returned via the OLDC system, the ILR is used:
- to monitor individual provider's delivery against provision plan or contract;
- to inform local decisions about plans and provision;
- to monitor progress to targets;
- to inform national planning, including policy development and modelling;
- to calculate actual funding earned;
- to monitor quality of provision and evaluate the effectiveness of providers across the learning and skills sector;
- to make the case to government for levels of funding appropriate to the sector;
- to demonstrate the outcomes of the distribution of funds.

ILR return deadlines (by 6pm on this date)				
Month and year	**Learner-responsive**		**Employer-responsive**	
	2009/10	**2010/11**	**2009/10**	**2010/11**
April 2010			8th (W08)	
May 2010	17th (F03)		7th (W09)	
June 2010			4th (W10)	
July 2010			6th (W11)	
August 2010			5th (W12)	
September 2010	6th (F04)			6th (ER01)
October 2010				6th (ER02)
November 2010	22nd (F05)		12th (W13)	4th (ER03)
December 2010		6th (LR01)		4th (ER04)
January 2011				7th (ER05)
February 2011		14th (LR02)		4th (ER06)
March 2011				4th (ER07)
April 2011				6th (ER08)
May 2011		16th (LR03)		6th (ER09)
June 2011				6th (ER10)
July 2011				6th (ER11)
August 2011				4th (ER12)
September 2011		5th (LR04)		
October 2011				
November 2011		21st (LR05)		11th (ER13)

Source: *ILR Specification 09/10 Appendix A* (v.4) and 10/11 (v.1), *the information authority*

Time from start

The reference dates that were used for funding and statistical purposes have now been replaced with a minimum attendance or 'time from start' period:

- learners enrolled on courses of 24 weeks would not be counted, if they withdrew within the first six weeks
- learners enrolled on courses of two weeks or more, but less than 24 weeks, would not be counted if they withdrew within the first two weeks
- learners enrolled on courses less than two weeks would not be counted, if they withdrew before attending once.

Employer-responsive in learning census dates

For each ER ILR return, only activity up to and including the last day of the previous month is taken into account. For example, the in-learning census date for the first ILR of the year (period one), returned on the fourth working day of September, would be the 31st August. The thirteenth and final ER ILR return is to be used by providers to ensure all activity is recorded, particularly achievements that occurred during the year.

ILR changes for 2010/11

The following changes were published in November 2009, and relate to the ILR for learner (LR) and employer-responsive (ER) provision.

Reduction of data fields:
- Two fields now blank, so null filled (L02 and H02);
- Four fields removed (L25, L44, A21 and A54);
- A02 removed for LR (but remains for ER).

Additional data fields:
- Eligibility for enhanced ER funding (A69), to be used instead of L28. Null values (00) should be used in A69 for all LR provision;
- Contracting organisation (A70) replaces L25. Eligible codes are found in Appendix E of the ILR Specification 2010/11;
- Qualification on entry (H45), replacing code H11 for new starts.

New aggregate data collections:
- A learner number return, by age, to be made before LR01 for Young People's Learning Agency (YPLA) funded enrolments. This will be collected on the first Monday in October;
- A report on employer contributions to be returned with ER12 or ER13;
- Publication of the final details planned for the end of March 2010.

Changes to data collection arrangements:
- The learner-responsive ILR data collection windows have shortened, and will be 'hard closed' at 6pm on deadline date (p.29);
- The ILR files have been renamed from F to LR for learner-responsive and W to ER for employer-responsive;
- All Independent Specialist Colleges will return an ILR;
- University for Industry (UfI) learndirect provision will return an LR ILR.

Changes to validation rules:
- ILR changes mean some of the validation rules change (p.84);
- Some of the Learning Aim Database (LAD) validation rules have changed due to the changes in funding policy rules;
- Increased validation for the Unique Learning Number (p.108).

Changes to existing learner fields:
- L28 re-named 'eligibility for 16–18 funding entitlement' and removed from ER collection (replaced by A69);
- Additional learner support (L29) has code 41 removed. All learners need to be re-coded with code 42 or 43 to identify learners with a Section 139A Learning Difficulty Assessment (previously know as a Section 140);
- Learner support reason (L34) has code 54 added for adult education bursary;
- Learner status on last working day before learning (L36) is not valid for aims starting in 10/11. Field A66 should be used.

Changes to existing aim fields:

- LSC funding stream model (A10) has two new codes added. Code 81 for 'Other SFA funding model' and code 82 for 'Other YPLA funding model'. Code 80 'Other LSC funding' remains for continuing learners.
- Source of funding (A11) has five new codes added. Code 105 for SFA, code 106 for YPLA, code 107 for local authority (YPLA funds), code 108 for local authority (adult safeguarded learning funds) which replaces code 026 and code 109 for local authority (other, not YPLA or adult safeguarded learning funds) which replaces code 027.
- Reason for full funding/co-funding of learning aim (A14) has code 12 (Tax relief for vocational programmes) removed.
- Programme type (A15) has a new code 19 for Foundation Learning Programmes to replace code 11–14 (to be used alongside codes 112–115 in A46 indicating intended destination). Also, Entry to Employment (E2E) code 09 should only be used for continuing learners.
- Main delivery method (A18) to be collected for all ER aims that start in 2010/11 alongside group and one-to-one hours data in A64 and A65 to support the setting of funding rates. Also, new code 24 added for learning in workplace which replaces code 22 and 23 for Train to Gain.
- Only UKPRN numbers (p.109) will be valid in A22.
- Completion status (A34) code 6 (learner has temporarily withdrawn from the aim due to an agreed break in learning) also made available for LR.
- Learning outcome (A35) has two new codes for achievement of AS levels/non-AS levels. Code 6 is for uncashed AS Levels and code 7 is for cashed AS levels.
- Proportion of funding remaining (A51a) now explicitly states it should not be used to vary funding rate when the full qualification is delivered.
- Source of tuition fees (A57) code 04 added for MoD Level 3 Entitlement.
- National skills academy (A63) code 14 added for Social care and code 15 added for Information Technology.

Changes to existing HE fields:

- The Highest Qualification on Entry field (H11) is not valid for new starters as the new H45 field should be used instead.

Future plans for the ILR beyond 2010/11

In December 2009 *the information authority* indicated that they plan to remove local monitoring fields (L41 and A47); develop a learner data strategy; inform developments such as the new Single Account Management System (SAMS); introduce Extensible Markup Language (XML) where beneficial; move to a single, combined ILR for 2011/12; consult to improve the use of existing data, as well as consider more fundamental reforms; the DCSF have tendered for a 14–19 management information strategy, which may impact on the plans above; also, the new 14–19 common application process (CAP) is likely to impact on the data that is requested from providers.

The Learning Aim Database

> The online LAD search engine will tell you whether a qualification is fundable and at what funding rate. Everyone involved in planning courses should know how to use it to not only find new qualifications, but to regularly check the status of existing ones. With the introduction of the Qualifications Credit Framework this is particularly important at the moment.
>
> Claire Arbery, Contracts Manager, City of Bristol College

From accreditation to the Learning Aim Database

The Learning Aim Database online

Learning aims

Other online qualification search engines

The Learning Aim Database (LAD) contains information about all recognised learning aims (such as qualifications and non-accredited courses) for England. It includes learning aim information required to complete The Individualised Learner Record (ILR) data returns, as well as funding and statistical data for use by the provider and others. It holds data for three teaching years and can be searched online or downloaded in a variety of formats. The collection of information within the LAD, and its maintenance, is the responsibility of the Data Service (p.104).

The diagram below shows how the LAD is a vital source of information used to calculate funding, record enrolments and report on performance.

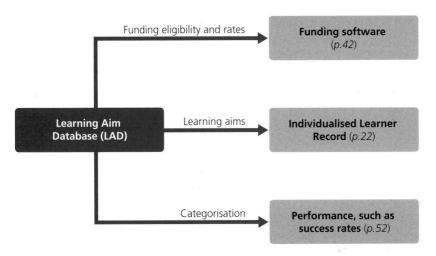

It is therefore critical that providers select the correct learning aim for each and every enrolment, and ensure an up-to-date version of the LAD is used.

Note

As a result of the UK Vocational Qualification Reform Programme (UKVQRP) and the introduction of the Qualifications and Credit Framework (QCF), many new learning aims are being introduced and existing ones are being phased out or replaced. Providers should consider whether they have sufficient resources focused on monitoring the availability and eligibility of new and existing learning aims.

This chapter explains the process by which newly accredited qualifications are approved for government funding, have funding rates applied, and then appear on the LAD. Providers can then use the online LAD search engine to find qualifications (p.36), along with their funding and statistical data (p.39). However, the LAD is not the only online qualification search engine, as explained on page 40.

From accreditation to the Learning Aim Database

The process required to make a newly accredited qualification available for funding is complex and potentially lengthy. Following accreditation it takes several stages to approve and set funding rates for the qualification. Until these have been agreed and made available on the Learning Aim Database, providers cannot claim funding for the relevant qualification.

Once the Office for the Qualifications and Examinations Regulator (OfQUAL) have accredited a qualification, it will be assigned a unique Qualification Accreditation Number (QAN). For example, 500/7916/5 is the QAN for a GCSE in Mathematics from Edexcel. This information can be viewed on the National Database of Accredited Qualifications (p.40). The qualification then follows two approval processes, one for young people and one for adults, before funding rates can be assigned. An eight-character learning aim is then set, which alongside the associated funding data is published by the Data Service on the Learning Aim Database.

Making an accredited qualification fundable

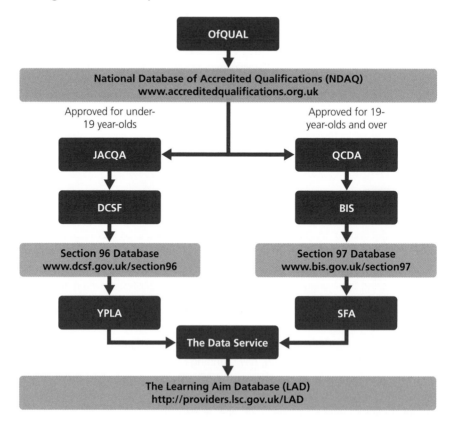

The Data Service has produced a useful step-by-step guide to help providers obtain the status of, and data for, many qualifications.

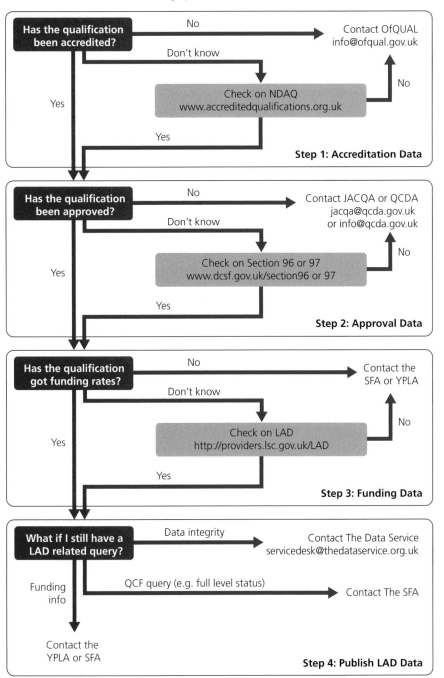

The Learning Aim Database online

The LAD is available as an online search engine. Whilst the search engine options are very detailed (see following page), this provides a lot of flexibility to find a qualification, or a group of qualifications.

Searching the LAD online

If, for example, you wanted a list of all the Level 2 qualifications accredited by Edexcel with the word 'beauty' in the title, then the LAD would be searched using the title, awarding body and Level fields as follows:

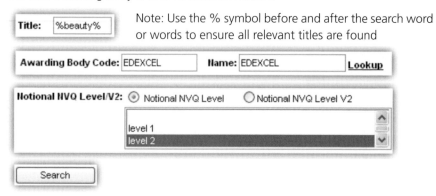

| Title: | %beauty% |

Note: Use the % symbol before and after the search word or words to ensure all relevant titles are found

Awarding Body Code: EDEXCEL   Name: EDEXCEL   Lookup

Notional NVQ Level/V2: ⦿ Notional NVQ Level   ○ Notional NVQ Level V2

level 1
level 2

Search

The LAD will then list the qualifications which match the search criteria:

Learning Aim	Learning Aim Title
10050644	BTEC Certificate in Retail Beauty Consultancy
50017305	BTEC Diploma in Retail Beauty Consultancy
00291905	First Diploma in Beauty Therapy (Provider Specific)
5004946X	Higher Diploma in Hair and Beauty Studies
50032690	NVQ in Beauty Therapy

At this stage the LAD will also list which qualification is fundable for learner-responsive (LR) provision (those aged 16–18 and/or 19+), as well as for employer-responsive provision (Apprenticeships and Train to Gain).

Learning Aim	Fundable in 2009/10? (as at 08/03/10)			
	16–18 LR	19+ LR	Apprenticeships	Train to Gain
10050644	Yes	Yes	Yes	No
50017305	Yes	Yes	No	Yes
00291905	No	No	No	No
5004946X	Yes	Yes	No	No
50032690	Yes	Yes	Yes	Yes

The online LAD search engine

http://providers.lsc.gov.uk/LAD/aims/searchcriteria.asp

Learning aims

Every qualification, at every level, and from each awarding body, has a unique eight-character learning aim. Non-accredited provision also requires a learning aim (see generic learning aim section below), which is why learning aims are not simply called qualification accreditation numbers.

Providers must accurately record in field A09, within the Individualised Learner Record (ILR), the planned learning aim for each and every enrolment (p.23). Colleges with learner-responsive provision must also record the learning aims for those enrolments which attract no government funding.

Each learning aim has detailed information held within the LAD, including funding rates in the form of standard learner number (SLNs) and programme weightings (see following page). However, even if the LAD shows a qualification as fundable, the relevant funding guidance must be consulted to ensure both learner and provider eligibility.

Programme aims

Learners enrolled on Apprenticeships or Personalised Learning Programmes within Foundation Learning are required to enrol on a programme aim (ZPROG001) in addition to the individual learning aims. The new 14–19 Diplomas also require an over-arching programme aim.

Generic learning aims

In some cases, such as for non-certificated provision or for units, credits and other partial qualifications, a generic learning aim is required. Details of how to use generic aims can be found within Appendix H of the ILR specification (p.24). Below is an example of a generic learning aim, and how it is made up:

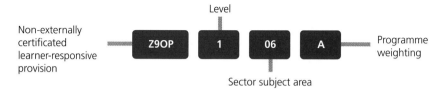

Annex H also includes learning aim details for particular programmes and funding sources, such as provision at long-term residential colleges.

> **Note**
>
> Learning aim details can be shared by pasting the LAD web address into an email, which is unique to each learning aim. Where applicable the LAD page will have an 'Ofqual details' link, which goes to the corresponding NDAQ webpage (p.40).

Selection of information for a qualification held on the LAD	
Learning aim reference	10050644
Learning aim title	BTEC Certificate in Retail Beauty Consultancy
Level	2
Awarding body	Edexcel
Accreditation end date	31/08/2010
Certification end date	31/08/2012
16–18 and 19+ learner-responsive SLN glh	150
16–18 and 19+ learner-responsive programme weighting	C (1.3)
Apprenticeship SLN	0.333
Apprenticeship employer contribution	45.6%
Apprenticeship programme weighting	A (1.0)
Apprenticeship framework	The LAD includes functionality to view all the relevant qualifications within a framework
Whether or not a qualification contributes to a government target	No, this is not a full Level 2 qualification
Number of Qualifications and Credit Framework (QCF) credits	This qualification is not on the QCF
The sector subject area Tier 1	Retail and Commercial Enterprise (07)
The sector subject area Tier 2	Retailing and Wholesaling (0.71)
Sector Lead Body	Skillsmart Retail

Other online qualification search engines

As referred to on page 34, there are three other online government search engines which contain qualification information. The National Database of Accredited Qualifications (NDAQ) lists qualifications accredited by the Office of the Qualifications and Examinations Regulator (OfQUAL). The Section 96 and Section 97 search engines list those approved. However, it is only the Learning Aim Database which will confirm whether a qualification is eligible for government funding in England.

The National Database of Accredited Qualifications
www.accreditedqualifications.org.uk

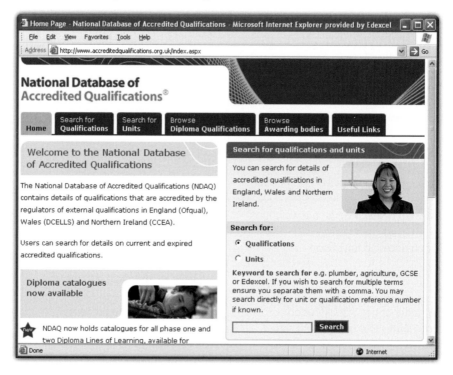

The NDAQ is particularly useful, not only because qualification information appears here before going on the Learning Aim Database (LAD), but because it includes additional information, such as:
- a qualification summary, with progression and potential job occupations;
- the grading system and assessment methods;
- additional requirements and/or exemptions;
- mandatory and optional units, including rules of combination;
- qualification structure, with detailed information about units, such as: the unit owner; credit value; learning outcomes and assessment criteria.

The Section 96 and 97 qualifications
www.dcsf.gov.uk/section96 and www.bis.gov.uk/section97

The Learning and Skills Act 2000 refers to approved qualifications which providers in England can offer to those under and over 19 years of age. Section 96 covers qualifications for those under the age of 19, and Section 97 covers qualifications approved for learners aged 19 years and older.

The relevant Secretary of State approves external qualifications having received advice from the Joint Advisory Committee for Qualifications Approval (JACQA) and Qualifications and Curriculum Development Agency (QCDA). Once approved the details will go on the Section 96 and/or Section 97 database (*p.34*).

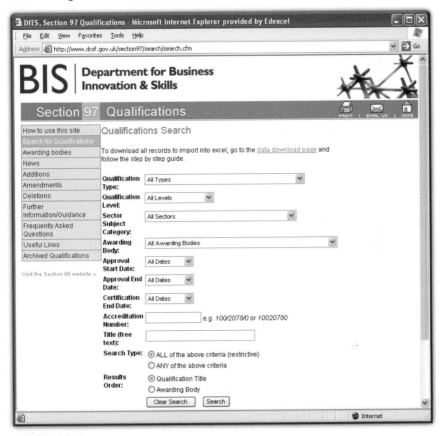

Note

After being added to NDAQ it can take several weeks for a qualification to be added to Section 96 or 97 (*p.34*). Also, as Section 97 of the Learning and Skills Act 2000 has been repealed, it is highly likely that the Section 97 website will be quickly phased out.

The Learner Information Suite

> The LIS is an incredibly useful piece of software for both colleges and training providers. It calculates funding, validates data and the database it produces can be linked to in-house software for more bespoke reporting.
>
> John Callaghan, Principal, North East Worcestershire College

Preparing the LIS for use

The LIS and learner-responsive provision

The LIS and employer-responsive provision

Advanced use of the LIS

The Learner Information Suite (LIS) is data validation and funding software which is used by all providers who return data using the online data collection (OLDC) system. The LIS is free to download from the internet and responsibility for managing it lies with the Data Service (p.104).

The LIS validates data for the following funding types:
- Learner-responsive (LR)
- Employer-responsive (ER)
- Adult safeguarded learning (ASL)
- European Social Fund short records (ESF SR)
- Learndirect (Ufi).

It also calculates derived data and generates reports on learner and funding volumes for learner-responsive provision (16–18 and 19+) as well as employer-responsive provision (Apprenticeships and Train to Gain).

The diagram below shows how data is imported into the LIS, which is then exported in the form of reports, or as a database.

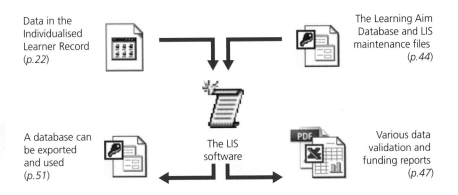

Providers use the LIS to produce funding reports and monitor their performance against targets. The LIS also validates data on the basis of the national ILR specification (p.24). Providers should therefore regularly check the validity of their data by using the LIS. The LIS database export is also required by providers when using the Data Self Assessment Toolkit (p.86). This chapter explains how to install and use the LIS.

Note

The LIS software is both important and very useful to providers, but it does have limitations. A small number of validation rules are not in the LIS and all funding values are indicative. The definitive validations and funding volumes are applied and reported by the OLDC system, after ILR data has been returned (p.28).

Preparing the LIS for use

Installing the LIS

The LIS software is freely available to download from the internet. At the time of writing the latest version of the LIS could be found at the web address below, alongside a variety of related files and user guides.

www.lsc.gov.uk/providers/Data/Software/LIS

Once the zipped LIS file has been downloaded and unzipped, the software can be installed in the usual fashion. For the LIS to work, Microsoft .NET Framework 2.0 is required, which is also freely available to download via the web address above.

Once installed, the LIS will appear as a program. Users will first need to log in. The password is *password*, which can be changed. Before data can be validated or funding calculated, the LIS now requires that four files are imported.

LIS maintenance

Four files need to be imported to ensure the LIS is up to date.

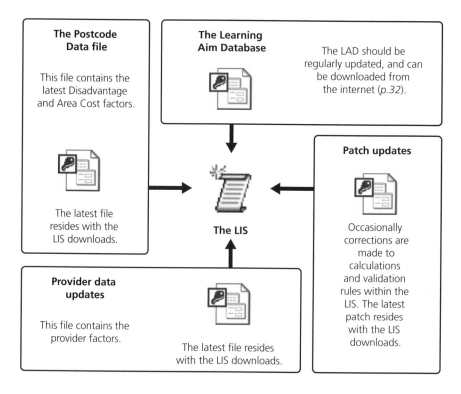

The Postcode Data file

This file contains the latest Disadvantage and Area Cost factors.

The latest file resides with the LIS downloads.

The Learning Aim Database

The LAD should be regularly updated, and can be downloaded from the internet (*p.32*).

The LIS

Patch updates

Occasionally corrections are made to calculations and validation rules within the LIS. The latest patch resides with the LIS downloads.

Provider data updates

This file contains the provider factors.

The latest file resides with the LIS downloads.

The Learning Aim Database (LAD) contains the funding and statistical data which the LIS uses to validate enrolments and derive the correct funding values. The latest LAD should be downloaded from the internet for the relevant year and imported via the Batch Import screen (see below). ━━━━━━━

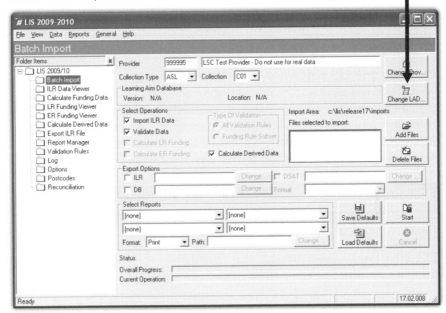

The remaining three maintenance files are updated less frequently than the LAD, and reside on the web as LIS software downloads. All three files need to be imported via the Maintenance tab within the LIS Options screen.

The provider data file and patch updates are imported separately via the Update Data button. ━━━━━

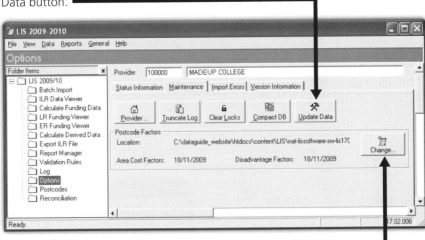

The postcode file is imported by clicking on the change button. ━━━━

The LIS and learner-responsive provision

Before learner-responsive (LR) data can be submitted it must be valid, which means it conforms to a national data specification (*p.24*). The LIS should be used by LR providers before submitting data to check that all their data is valid. The LIS also calculates LR funding and some performance measures, which can be read as a report or exported as data.

Running the LIS software

After the LIS has imported the latest LAD and maintenance files (*p.45*), the relevant provider needs to be selected. The LIS is now ready to validate data and calculate funding for learner-responsive (LR) provision. Firstly, an Individualised Learner Record (ILR) file needs to be imported into the LIS. In the example below, an LR F01 collection type has been selected, then F01 ILR text file can be imported.

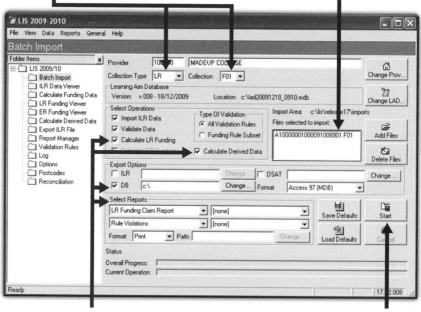

The funding calculations, derived data and database export can be selected and up to four reports pre-selected before pressing start.

If the ILR data does not successfully import then refer to the LIS user guide and if necessary consult any relevant internal IT support. Failing this, email servicedesk@thedataservice.org.uk for assistance.

Once the ILR has imported the LIS, validation and funding reports can be produced from the Report Manager screen.

LIS data validation reports

The most important LIS reports are those that validate the ILR data. Within the Report Manager screen, report reference number one is the most comprehensive, as it lists the details of any 'rule violations' found in an ILR.

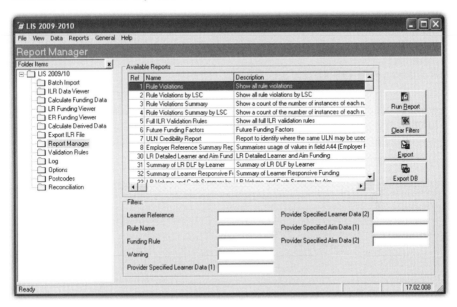

There are 46 different LIS validation rules which highlight fundable errors. For example, validation rule A27_A31_1 will list enrolments with an actual end date before the start date. When a fundable error occurs the LIS will not generate any funding for the relevant enrolment. The LIS also applies 490 validation rules which highlight non-fundable errors. For example, validation rule A31_2 will list enrolments with actual end dates after the date the data was produced. When a non-fundable error occurs the LIS will still calculate funding, although the data will need to be corrected before it can be submitted.

The validation reports also contain warnings. The LIS applies 61 validation rules which list warnings. For example, A27_L11_3 will list enrolments for learners aged 100 years old or over. Much like DSAT reports (p.86), warnings should be checked as although they conform to the national data specification they flag potential errors. A small number of data collection validation rules are not in the LIS. A list of these can be found alongside the LIS documents on the internet.

LIS funding reports

The LIS includes several funding reports which apply the national funding rates and relevant provider factor. The LR Funding Claim Report (reference number 35) includes both 16–18 and 19+ learner and funding volumes. The figures from this report are used by providers to submit an in-year, year-end and final funding claim.

The LIS and employer-responsive provision

Employer-responsive (ER) data must be valid, which means it conforms to national data rules. Once valid, it can be returned to the funding body via the online data collections system (p.28). The LIS should be used by ER providers to find and then correct these errors. The LIS also calculates Apprenticeship and Train to Gain funding.

Running the LIS software

After the LIS has imported the latest LAD and maintenance files (p.44) the relevant provider needs to be selected. The LIS is now ready to validate data and calculate funding for employer-responsive (ER) provision. Firstly, an ILR file needs to be imported into the LIS. In the example below, an ER W07 collection type has been selected, then a W07 ILR text file can be imported.

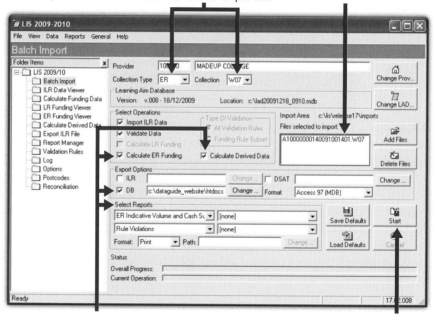

The funding and derived data calculations and a database export can be selected and up to four reports can be pre-selected, before pressing start.

If the ILR data does not successfully import then refer to the LIS user guide and if necessary consult any relevant internal IT support. Alternatively contact servicedesk@thedataservice.org.uk for assistance.

Once the ILR has imported the LIS, validation and funding reports can be produced from the Report Manager screen.

Data validation reports

The LIS validates the data and reports on rule violations for employer-responsive ILRs in the same way as for learner-responsive (p.47). Providers should regularly run the LIS data validation reports and correct all the rule violations (errors) before returning their monthly ER ILR.

ER data funding reports

The LIS contains a number of Apprenticeship and Train to Gain funding reports within the Report Manager screen. One of the most useful funding reports is the Indicative Volume and Cash Summary (report reference number 13 or 15). This report includes the funding for the year-to-date and the current period (month) for Apprenticeships by age, level and framework and for Train to Gain by sector subject area.

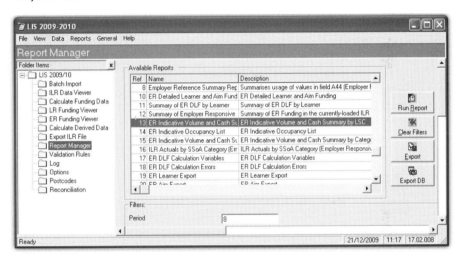

The funding detail for every Apprenticeship and Train to Gain enrolment is listed in the ER Indicative Occupancy List (report reference number 14). This report is exported as a spreadsheet and is similar to the Provider Funding Report (PFR) that can downloaded from the online data collections system after each monthly ILR return (p.28). All the LIS funding reports state that they are 'indicative' and that the PFR contains the definitive funding values.

Note

The LIS ER funding reports contain a filter which enables providers to select a period. For example, period eight would include all on-programme funding from August to the following March. Period 12 would include all on-programme payments for the entire academic year. Providers can use this LIS feature to help them forecast future funding commitments for existing enrolments (excluding additional funding for achievements or reductions due to withdrawals).

Advanced use of the LIS

The LIS is an important tool as all providers should be using it to check and help validate their LR and ER ILR data before making a funding claim. However, the LIS also calculates funding and derives a significant amount of additional data. For example, the LIS will derive a learner's age by applying the relevant rules (which differ between LR and ER) to their date of birth. More importantly, this derived data is readily accessible from tables within a database, which can be exported from the LIS.

This database gives the provider the ability to enhance their own reports.

Provider software

The provider will record data about the course, student, enrolments and attendance within their system. From here an ILR file will be exported.

Individualised Learner Record

The ILR text file contains the nationally prescribed dataset, as required for claiming both LR and ER funding (p.22). This can be imported into the LIS.

Learner Information Suite software

The LIS applies data validation and funding calculations to the ILR data. A database containing this derived validation and funding data can be exported.

Learner Information Suite database export

The LIS database contains raw and derived data within tables (see next page). The tables can be imported or linked to other systems.

Provider reporting system

The provider can import the tables into their own reporting system. At this stage linkages can be made to data not in the ILR, such as provider course titles.

Provider reports

The provider can produce validation and funding reports from their own reporting system. This might include the total funding for each course code and title.

The LIS database

The LIS database tables contain raw data about funding, derived data calculations and validation. It also has tables linked from a Learning Aim Database extract, ILR lookup codes, tables of information required by the LIS to run, tables of results of LIS functions and structural tables. The picture below shows all the ER database tables as they appear in MS Access.

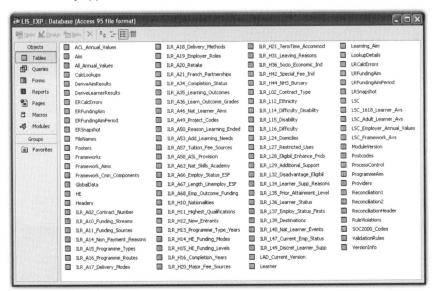

The following four documents are available to download from the internet alongside the LIS software.

- User guidance (88 pages);
- Database guidance (8 pages);
- Report guidance (108 pages);
- Technical specification of funding calculations (132 pages).

These four documents are particularly useful to management information staff and software developers, since they explain:

- all the functions and filters within the LIS;
- table names, their source and definition;
- information about reports, including the Summary Statement of Activity;
- warnings where derived value calculations may be incorrect;
- the way in which the LIS calculates both LR and ER funding.

Note

A register of known issues is also available on the internet alongside the LIS software. Users should ensure they are aware of these, and that at all times they are using the last version of the LIS for the relevant year.

Success rates and MLPs

> Close analysis of framework achievement rates and benchmarking have informed our drive to significantly improve success rates for construction apprentices.
>
> Max Hamps, Director of Training Provision, ConstructionSkills

Learner-responsive success rates

Employer-responsive success rates

Minimum Levels of Performance (MLP)

Identifying and managing underperformance

Success rates are calculated using a nationally-consistent methodology and provide a key attainment measure for the sector. They are expressed as a percentage. For example, if the success rate was 80% this would mean that eight out of ten learners who started a qualification had passed (achieved a successful outcome). The success rate is also the retention rate (number completed divided by number started) multiplied by the achievement rate (number achieved divided by number completed).

Retention, achievement and success rates are used by:
- providers to assess quality, set targets, monitor performance and as supporting evidence within self-assessment reports (p.98);
- commissioners, such as local authorities, to identify high-performing providers as well as to manage underperformance (p.60);
- the Skills Funding Agency and Young People's Learning Agency (YPLA) as part of the funding methodology;
- Ofsted to help inform its judgements and grades (p.96);
- Government departments to measure performance (p.16).

Introduction to the success rate methodology

Success rate methodologies have been developed by the LSC and are published by the Data Service (p.104), and there has been significant change for 2008/09. Primarily this has been to the definition of a start, which determines which enrolments are included in success rate calculations. Only those enrolments that are funded will be counted, some qualifications are excluded, and the learner- and employer-responsive funding methodologies apply a new qualifying period. Enrolments withdrawn within the qualifying period are not counted.

Course duration	Qualifying period
24 weeks or more	Six weeks
2 to less than 24 weeks	Two weeks
Less than 2 weeks	One attendance

Example retention, achievement and success rates		
18 stay on programme beyond the qualifying period	18 starts	
16 of the 18 starts complete	16 completed	89% retention rate
14 of the 16 achieve the qualification	14 achieved	88% achievement rate
So, 14 of the 18 starts were successful	14 succeeded	78% success rate

Minimum Levels of Performance (MLP) are weighted success rates with thresholds which are used by providers and commissioners for the purposes of identifying and managing underperformance (p.58).

Learner-responsive success rate reports

The Data Service publish provider learner-responsive Qualification Success Rate (QSR) reports. These are accessible from the Provider Gateway (*p.15*). The 2008/09 QSR reports shows the number of learning aims (enrolments) achieved, expressed as a percentage of the number that were started and expected to be achieved during the 2008/09 academic year. QSR reports should be used by providers to help them assess the quality of the courses they provide. At a more detailed level, a spreadsheet is included alongside the QSR report which includes all the enrolment records and success rates. Many providers will also use their own software to analyse and monitor success rates, such as ProAchieve (*p.23*).

Learner-responsive QSR reports

The learner-responsive QSR reports for 2008/09 are calculated using the learner-responsive Individualised Learner Record (ILR) data supplied by the provider in the final (F05) collection for 2008/09 (*p.29*), and four previous academic years. The precise calculation method is published on the Data Service website.

Summary of 2008/09 learner-responsive QSR reports:
- they include the 2006/07, 2007/08 and 2008/09 success rate and volume of starts for long and short aims, by age (16–18 and 19+), by level, and by sector subject area (*p.57*);
- they only include learner-responsive funded learners;
- they exclude learners under the age of 16 on 31 August of the academic year when they started the aim;
- they exclude Key and Functional Skills qualifications from the main reports, although their success rates are shown in a separate table.

The QSR report also includes success rate tables for:
- all qualifications by age and long (24 weeks or more) and all short;
- all long qualifications by age and level;
- long qualifications by age (excluding A-level qualifications, AS and A2);
- long qualification by age for A-level qualifications, AS and A2;
- all qualifications by gender and age;
- all qualifications by ethnicity and age;
- all qualifications by Learning Difficulties and Disabilities and age;
- full Level 2 and full Level 3 qualifications by age;
- all Skills for Life qualifications by age;
- all Functional Skills qualifications by Level and age;
- all Key Skills qualifications by Level and age.

The QSR report also has retention and achievement tables for long and short aims by age, Level by age, short (five to less than 24 weeks) and very short (less than five weeks) aims by age; sector subject area by age; full Level 2 and full Level 3 by age and Skills for Life by age.

The 2008/09 modified success rate calculation

As shown in the image below (from page 1 of a 2008/09 learner-responsive QSR report), the figures for 2006/07 and 2007/08 are also included alongside 2008/09, as are national averages for 2008/09.

Success Rate (Learner Responsive)			

Provider:	MADEUP COLLEGE	All Qualifications (excluding Functional and Key Skills)			
Organisation Type:	General FE College incl Tertiary	Percentiles: (2008/09)	25th	50th	75th
LSC Region:	Greater London	Success Rate:	73.6 %	77.5 %	80.5 %
Lead Local LSC:	London North	Retention Rate:	84.6 %	87.0 %	89.2 %
		Achievement Rate:	86.7 %	89.5 %	91.3 %

1. Headline Actual Performance (excluding Functional and Key Skills)

		2006/07	2007/08	2008/09	National
All Long	Starts	15,400	14,779	11,520	1,475,238
	Success Rate	76.9 %	78.6 %	75.6 %	74.1 %
All Short	Starts	9,805	11,272	8,807	691,994
	Success Rate	87.6 %	87.4 %	85.7 %	84.0 %
Total	Starts	25,205	26,051	20,327	2,167,232
	Success Rate	81.0 %	82.4 %	80.0 %	77.2 %

However, the calculation method for learner-responsive success rates has been modified for 2008/09, whilst the 2006/07 and 2007/08 figures remain calculated using the original method. In the main, the modifications are designed to better align (harmonise) the success rate calculation with the demand-led funding formula that was introduced in 2008/09. The most significant modification has been to the definition of a start, so that only funded enrolments will be included within the success rate calculation (p.53). The impact of the modifications will vary by provider, and this means that care should be taken when using the QSR to compare 2008/09 success rates with previous years. For further information and advice refer to the latest Data Service and Ofsted guidance.

> Success rate methodologies are only true currencies for the year in which they are calculated and whilst, for information purposes, it is sometimes useful to see trend data using the latest method, this can be misleading.
>
> Source: *Success Rate News*, the Data Service (December 2009)

Key and functional skills

Key and functional skills qualifications are excluded from the main QSR and Minimum Levels of Performance (MLP) reports (p.58), unless they are part of an Apprenticeship. However, all functional skills qualifications are likely to be included in QSR and MLP reports once they fully replace key skills, which is expected to be in 2010/11. Further changes are likely, and *the information authority* (p.106) have published a success rate timetable on their website. This includes the rationale for changes as well as any predicted impact, if known: http://tinyurl.com/yax6tmz

Employer-responsive success rate reports

The Data Service publish quarterly provider Qualification Success Rate (QSR) reports for Train to Gain and Apprenticeships. Both reports are accessible from the Provider Gateway (p.15), and have been calculated using the employer-responsive Individualised Learner Record (p.22). QSR reports should be used by providers to help them assess the quality of the qualifications they provide. Many providers will also use their own software to analyse and monitor success rates.

Overall and timely success rates

Train to Gain and Apprenticeship success rates are reported using two measures; overall and timely. 'Overall' counts all learning aim achievements over time, with reporting taking place in the year that they are finished. However, timely success rates only count those achievements that are completed within 30 days (2008/09) or 90 days (2009/10) of the initial planned end date, which means it is time-dependent.

Apprenticeship Framework 2008/09 QSR reports

The only Apprenticeship outcome that is counted as a success is one in which all qualifications within the learner's relevant framework has been achieved. This is known as a Framework Success Rate, which for 2008/09 and the previous three academic years is published for overall and timely.

The Apprenticeship QSR report zipped file contains:
- a summary report covering timely and overall Level 2 and Level 3 framework success rates for England and for each region and local authority in which the provider has delivered Apprenticeships;
- detailed separate reports for England, regions and local authorities (where applicable, relating to the provider), by sector subject area (p.57) and sector framework code (SFC);
- a spreadsheet of success rates details for all learners (relating to the provider).

Example Apprenticeship QSR summary report

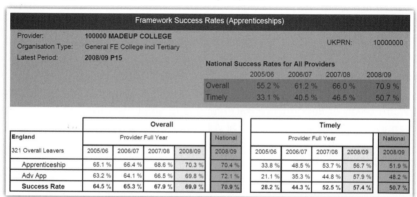

Train to Gain Framework 2008/09 QSR reports

Train to Gain QSR reports show the number of qualifications achieved, the number of leavers and the success rates (broken down by type of qualification and sector subject area) by region for 2008/09 and the previous three years. The national figures for 2008/09 are also listed. For 2009/10, changes have been made to the calculation of Train to Gain success rates to take into account the 'roll-on, roll-off' nature of the provision. In common with Apprenticeships, both an overall and timely (90-day cap) success rate are published in the quarterly QSR report.

Which to use, overall or timely?

In the case of both Train to Gain and Apprenticeships, the stated intention is to continue to capture all successful outcomes, even those that are outside a specified time period. Therefore the overall national success rate will be higher than the timely success rate. However, it is likely that Ofsted will pay most attention to the timely measure, which rewards providers that manage their provision well. Also, performance indicators, such as Minimum Levels of Performance (p.58), are likely in future to use the timely measure. Therefore many providers will set challenging but achievable targets based on the relevant timely success rate measure.

Sector subject areas

Sector subject areas (SSAs) are a classification system created by the Qualifications and Curriculum Authority (QCA). These are used within QSR reports for both learner- and employer-responsive provision to categorise the provision. The SSA is captured from the learning aim (p.39).

SSA number	Sector subject area (SSA)
1	Health, Public Services and Care
2	Science and Mathematics
3	Agriculture, Horticulture and Animal Care
4	Engineering and Manufacturing Technologies
5	Construction, Planning and the Built Environment
6	Information and Communication Technology
7	Retail and Commercial Enterprise
8	Leisure, Travel and Tourism
9	Arts, Media and Publishing
10	History, Philosophy and Theology
11	Social Sciences
12	Languages, Literature and Culture
13	Education and Training
14	Preparation for Life and Work
15	Business, Administration and Law

The 15 SSAs above are tier one SSAs, within which tier two SSAs are categorised (for example, in SSA 6 for ICT there are two tier two SSAs, 6.1 is for ICT Practitioners and 6.2 is for ICT Users).

Minimum Levels of Performance

Minimum levels of performance (MLP) reports were introduced in 2006. They consist of success rates, with various performance thresholds for provision by duration, level and funding type. They are used by the commissioning agencies to identify and manage underperforming provision (IMUP) (*p.60*). The MLP described here are applied in 2009/10, using 2008/09 success rates to inform 2010/11 commissioning decisions. MLP reports for both learner- and employer-responsive provision are downloaded from the secure Provider Gateway.

Learner-responsive MLP

The learner-responsive MLP thresholds applied to 2008/09 weighted success rates are:

Learner-responsive thresholds	Long (24 weeks+)	Short (5–24 weeks)	Very Short (<5 weeks)
A levels (A2 and A). AS level excluded	75%	62%	85%
Below Level 4	60%	62%	85%
Level 4 and above	58%	62%	85%
Unknown	60%	62%	85%

Learner-responsive MLP reports summarise the percentage of a provider's provision below the appropriate weighted success rate thresholds. A red cell indicates that a provider's provision is below the given threshold. A green cell indicates that provision is equal to or above the threshold. The report includes weighted success rates, guided learning hours (GLH), starts and associated funding by subject sector areas (*p.57*) by age (16–18 and 19+).

The last part of the learner-responsive MLP report lists the results for groups of individual qualifications ('map code level'), for example:

SSA 08 Level 1	Weighted success rate	GLH	Starts	Associated funding
Certificate in Coaching	58.2%	640	21	£6,465

The course above would be shaded yellow if the sector subject area by level is above the threshold overall, but there were pockets of underperformance at the qualification (map code) level. Providers can use these map code level reports as evidence in self-assessments reports (*p.98*), although they do not show the split between 16–18 and 19+.

Employer-responsive MLP

The employer-responsive MLP thresholds applied to 2008/09 success rates are:

Employer-responsive MLP thresholds	
Apprenticeships (full framework)	50%
Train to Gain	65%

There are separate MLP reports for Apprenticeship and Train to Gain provision, but they both highlight the provider's provision which falls below the relevant success rate threshold. A red cell indicates that the success rate is below the threshold and a green cell indicates that the success rate is equal to or above the threshold.

Apprenticeship reports include 16–18, 19–24 and 25+ success rates and number of leavers for Apprenticeships (Level 2) and Advanced Apprenticeships (Level 3) by sector subject area, sector framework code and by delivery location (region and local authority with a minimum of ten enrolments).

Train to Gain MLP reports include the success rates for the qualification types by region and local authority, as shown in the example below:

Train to Gain - Minimum Level of Performance Report Provider Summary – 2008/09

This report summarises the provider's provision which falls below the success rate thresholds of 65 %. A red cell indicates that the success rate is below 65 % and a green cell that the success rate is 65 % or greater.

* For these Local Authorities there is no Sector Subject Area analysis as the number of aims is less than ten.

MADEUP COLLEGE (100000) Greater London UKPRN: 10000000

Region	Local Authority	FLT	Skills for Life	Full Level 2	Full Level 3	Other	Overall
All Regions			41.4 %	65.5 %	73.0 %	91.3 %	69.6 %
Greater London				58.8 %	88.2 %		78.4 %
	Camden*				33.3 %		33.3 %

The Train to Gain MLP reports also include success rates by sector subject areas for both tier one and tier two (p.57) and the number of leavers for each of the local authorities in which delivery took place.

Note

Success rates in employer-responsive MLP reports are the same as those in QSR reports (p.54). However, success rates in learner-responsive MLP reports differ from those in QSR reports as they have been 'weighted' using expected guided learning hours for each enrolment. The resulting weighting is most heavily influenced by those programmes with the highest guided learning hours.

Identifying and managing underperformance

The relevant funding body will use performance measures to intervene, set improvement schedules and indicators and ultimately decommission provision. At present four types of provider performance are typically used for the purposes of intervention:

1. Minimum levels of performance (*p.58*)
2. Financial health, management and control (*p.79*)
3. Inspection outcomes (*p.96*)
4. Learner health, safety and welfare arrangements.

Where underperformance is minimal, it is expected that the provider will determine its own quality-improvement indicators as part of its self-assessment process [*p.98*]. The LSC will still agree actions with providers (or, where necessary, set improvement indicators) if there are concerns about performance. These improvement indicators will form part of the funding agreement or contract, and the timescales for achievement will be achievable and realistic. Failure to achieve them could result in the loss of funding for the specified provision.

Source: *Identifying and Managing Underperformance*, LSC (December 2009)

1. Minimum levels of performance (MLP)

The MLP for learner- and employer-responsive funding are explained in some detail on pages 58 and 59. For employer-responsive provision (Train to Gain and Apprenticeships) the MLP thresholds will inform commissioning and contract management decisions. However, in the case of learner-responsive provision, if insufficient provision is above the threshold a provider is served with a formal Notice To Improve (NTI). An NTI will be triggered if 15% or more of all long or short provision is below the MLP threshold (and will be sent to the governing body or equivalent when 25% or more is below the threshold). The NTI will include a schedule outlining the timeframe within which improvements need to be demonstrated. If the required improvements are not achieved within the timeframe the funding could cease, and might result in the funding body seeking an alternative provider via open competitive tendering.

Example MLP learner-responsive summary reports

Region	Local LSC	Provider Type	Provider Name	Long	Short	V. Short
Greater London						
	London North					
		General FE College incl Tertiary				
			MADEUP COLLEGE (100000)			
			% provision below threshold	7.6 %	26.7 %	5.9%
			Glh below threshold	132,643	12,583	48
			Total glh	1,746,429	47,059	807

The 26.7% of provision below the short course threshold in this report would trigger an NTI.

2. Financial health, management and control

Colleges in financial failure (graded inadequate in relation to financial health and/or financial management and control) usually trigger an NTI. The NTI may include a schedule requiring improvement in financial health over a three year period, or the addressing of financial management and control weaknesses within 12 months.

> The degree of financial intervention required for a particular college (and expressed in an NTI or agreed improvement indicators) will depend on the nature, scale and causes of the financial difficulties, and the stage at which they are identified. Once the funding body identifies actual or emerging financial difficulties, non-intervention is not an acceptable response.
>
> Source: *Identifying and Managing Underperformance*, LSC (December 2009)

3. Inspection outcomes

As a consequence of Ofsted inspection judgements, the funding body may seek to limit or cap growth in areas, or withdraw the contract. Where a provider is underperforming, with provision graded as inadequate, the funding body and provider, as part of the post-inspection action plan, will agree robust and binding improvement indicators as part of the conditions of funding. If the inspection judgement is satisfactory overall, but inadequate against one or more of the key areas (*p.97*), growth at an institutional level may be restricted. In all cases where Ofsted judges a college to be inadequate overall, the funding body will issue an NTI. Where Ofsted judges a college to be inadequate overall for a second time following re-inspection, that college will have failed the basic condition of its NTI.

4. Learner health, safety and welfare arrangements

> Failure to meet the required legislation, or guidelines such as the Protection of Vulnerable Adults, may also lead to the withdrawal of a contract. Where necessary, other provider types delivering to vulnerable learners must also meet these requirements. Failure to do so may also lead to the withdrawal of funding or a contract. Failure to meet the requirements in respect of safeguarding is now a limiting factor in inspection, and may also lead to withdrawal of funding [*p.97*].
>
> Source: *Identifying and Managing Underperformance*, LSC (December 2009)

Note

There is a difference in the accountability arrangements between independent training providers and colleges as a result of their different contractual relationship with the funding body. Specifically, independent training providers are managed in accordance with the terms of the contract, and would therefore not receive NTIs.

Learner progress

The data included in the Individualised Learner Record, Individual Learning Plans and the Learner Achievement Tracker are essential to help drive performance of learners through tutorials and drive up success.

Rachel Jones, Vice Principal Resources, Burton College

Value Added overview

The Learner Achievement Tracker

Value Added reports

Contextualised Value Added

The traditional approach to using qualification information for the purposes of measuring performance has been the use of achievement and success rates (p.52). However, these attainment measures do not take account of the actual grade that a learner has achieved, nor the level of improvement that they have made over time. This is important information, not least because it can help set stretching but attainable learner goals, as well as demonstrating how successful a provider is at progressing learners between qualification levels (adding value). For example, if a learner achieved three grade Ds at A-level this would be a pass and in success rate terms recorded as full achievement. However, if this learner had previously achieved all grade As for GCSE this would suggest that the learner has made less progress than might have initially been expected, and hence the provider had added less value. Similarly, providers whose learners enrol with low grades at GCSE and who go on to achieve high grades at A-level would expect to be recognised for the grade improvements that they have supported the learners in achieving.

In response to the need for a learner progress measure, and originally as part of the Government's 2005 Success for all Strategy, the Learning and Skills Council (LSC) developed Value Added (VA) reports for learners aged 16–18. The VA reports are designed to show how much qualification progress individual learners have made, based on their prior attainment compared to the national average. VA reports, which are accessible from the Learner Achievement Tracker (LAT), include Level 3 graded qualifications such as A-levels and BTEC National Diplomas (p.66).

The VA measures are useful as they can be used by:
- providers, to help them assess and improve their performance based on information about learner progress at subject, qualification, and subject sector area levels;
- Ofsted, to inform their initial ideas on the progress of learners, and to support judgement about provider performance;
- the Department for Children, Schools and Families (DCSF) and other stakeholders to inform policy-making and performance monitoring.

Source: *Learner Achievement Tracker Handbook 2007/08* LSC (February 2008)

The VA reports from the LAT are not the only learner progress reports available to providers. The Contextual Value Added (CVA) reports from the DCSF (p.70) produce an institution value added score. There are also privately run value added systems which some providers use, such as the Advanced Level Information System (ALIS) and the Advanced Level Performance System (ALPS).

There have also been types of learner progress reports produced in previous years which considered a broader range of Levels and qualifications, such as those called 'distance travelled'. However, the calculations for these reports are fraught with complexity, and at present the main focus for learner progress reporting is for 16–18s at Level 3.

Value Added overview

Value Added (VA) reports aim to show the progress of individual 16–18-year-old learners relative to the average progress made by similar learners nationally for the same qualification and subject, taking prior attainment into account.

Statistical analysis has shown that prior attainment is the best predictor of future performance in post-16 qualifications for learners in this age group. A calculation based on prior attainment that compares learner performance for a given subject and qualification helps us to:

- predict learner attainment and, on the basis of the expected attainment, establish target grades (or pass rates) to which learners and providers may aspire;
- make judgements about whether learners at a particular provider are performing at, below, or above a nationally average group of learners taking the same qualification and subject, and having the same prior attainment.

Source: *VA and DT for 16–18 learners: LAT Handbook 2007/08*, LSC (February 2008)

VA scores

VA scores within charts, as reported by the Learner Achievement Tracker (LAT) (*p.66*), compare the expected outcome of a learner based on their prior attainment at Key Stage 4 (such as GCSEs) with the grade they actually achieved at Level 3. Where a learner achieves a grade above the expected outcome this produces a positive VA score (and vice versa).

VA confidence intervals

The VA charts (*p.68*) also contain confidence intervals, which graphically show the range of scores for 95% of the learners. If both the VA score and the VA confidence interval is positive, the provider has greater confidence that their performance is higher than the national average.

QCA points and prior attainment

The Qualifications and Curriculum Authority (QCA), replaced in 2009 by the Qualifications and Curriculum Development Agency (QCDA), developed a system for assigning point scores to the grades for qualifications approved for 14–19-year-old learners. Prior attainment is calculated by adding together the total QCA points attained for applicable qualifications, and dividing the total size of the qualifications completed by the learner. This point scoring system is used to measure achievement in all qualifications included within VA, and to measure prior attainment. For some LAT outputs, QCA points have been split into bands. For example, national changes charts used banded prior attainment to indicate the expected performance of a learner for a range of prior attainment (*p.69*). The Prior Attainment Calculator can be used to determine QCA points (*p.65*).

Prior attainment calculator

The Prior Attainment Calculator converts a learner's prior attainment into a points score, and is available from the menu list on the LAT (*p.66*). Therefore, the calculator can be used to estimate a learner's probable level of attainment if they undertake a specific qualification. For example, providers can use it to calculate the learner's prior attainment, and then compare this to the national pattern for the qualification that the learner is proposing to take to assess their probable level of attainment.

As shown in the image of the Prior Attainment Calculator below, on the basis of qualification types and grades being added or removed from a list, the total and average point scores are displayed.

Learner Achievement Tracker > Prior Attainment Calculator		
Qualification : GCSE Short Course	Grade : A	
Qualification	**Grade**	**Points**
Key Skill at Level 2	P	34.50
Key Skill at Level 1	P	18.75
GCSE Full Course	B	46.00
GCSE Short Course	A	26.00
	Total Points Score	125.25
	Average Prior Attainment (QCA Points)	41.75

VA data sources, checking and calculation

The data used to calculate the VA measures and produce reports are obtained directly from awarding bodies. This attainment data is matched to attainment information for pre-16 qualifications, and then sent to providers as part of the DCSF's Achievement and Attainment Tables (AAT) checking exercise. Providers have an opportunity to amend the data, which is then credibility checked. The data is then fed into software to calculate average national performance, which is then fed into the LAT calculation engine, where provider VA scores based on the national data set are calculated.

The future of VA reports

The first VA reports were published by the LSC in 2005, and in April 2007 a review by the National Foundation for Educational Research (NFER) concluded that "by and large the system has been developed to high technical standards and is fit for purpose". More recently Christine Gilbert, Her Majesty's Chief Inspector (HMCI) at Ofsted, said she had "no doubt that value-added measures provided useful information showing how far pupils had progressed and how they compared with others elsewhere." (BBC News, http://tinyurl.com/ylbdjpw 18/12/09). Subject to resources, future reports may include additional factors such as gender, ethnicity and social background.

The Learner Achievement Tracker

The Learner Achievement Tracker (LAT) is the software for publishing value added reports and charts. The LAT is online, and can be accessed through the secure Provider Gateway. It has been maintained by the Data Service on behalf of the LSC.

Providers cannot view a report relating to another provider. However, authorised staff from other organisations can access all provider reports.

The LAT reports can be accessed by:
- Schools and sixth form colleges
- Further education colleges
- Local authorities
- Funding bodies, such as the Young People's Learning Agency
- Inspectorates, such as Ofsted.

The LAT suite of reports
The reports in the LAT are updated in the autumn of each year, and consist of three main report types.

LAT report type (p.68)	Report description
Summary reports	Shows the value added score for a provider for a particular qualification, such as A-levels, and for each separate subject, such as mathematics or history. For each of these scores there is a 95% confidence interval shown together with the national standard deviation.
National comparison reports	These charts are a more detailed view of a qualification and subject. In addition to figures shown on the summary reports, they also show the expected outcome for each level of prior attainment (the 'national line'). The outcomes of individual learners are shown on the chart, and the value added by the provider is shown in terms of a 'provider line'. This can help highlight whether a provider's over or under performance mainly occurs for learners with high or low prior attainment.
Chances charts	This shows the likelihood of each grade being achieved for a particular level of prior attainment, and is produced separately for each qualification and subject.

Producing VA reports from the LAT

The LAT contains a menu list on the left-hand side of the page. From here the relevant report type can be selected (see pages 68 and 69).

The last option on the list is a section for training, which includes a detailed tutorial on how to navigate and use the LAT.

Once a report type has been selected, such as Summary Reports, the user is then presented with a measure and qualification drop-down list.

The measure and qualification drop-down lists (see below) enable users to select the values that they wish to be included within the report. The values available to select will vary between providers, as they related to the particular courses that they delivered. Once the View Report button is pressed, the data tables and charts will be displayed on screen.

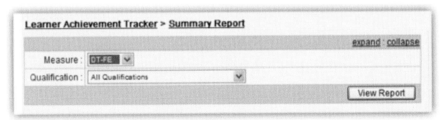

Source: *VA and DT for 16–18 learners: LAT Handbook 2007/08*, LSC (February 2008)

The reports can then be exported in the following formats:
- Acrobat (PDF) file
- Spreadsheet file that opens in Microsoft Excel
- TIFF file that opens in Microsoft Document Imaging
- Web archive file (an MHTML file that opens in Windows Explorer).

Note

Many of the tables and charts are complex and can take considerable time to understand. Critically, users need to know how to interpret the results in order to take appropriate action (such as investing additional support). The latest LAT Handbook contains detailed guidance and worked examples, which help users interpret VA results.

Value Added reports

A range of reports containing tables and charts can be generated from the Learner Achievement Tracker (LAT) (p.66). Examples of value added charts from these reports are shown and summarised on these two pages.

Value Added summary reports

VA summary reports and charts from the LAT show:

- For each provider, the VA scores for each qualification type
- For each qualification type, the VA scores for each subject, as well as an overall qualification score (see A-level example below)
- For all qualifications, the VA scores for each sector subject area (p.57).

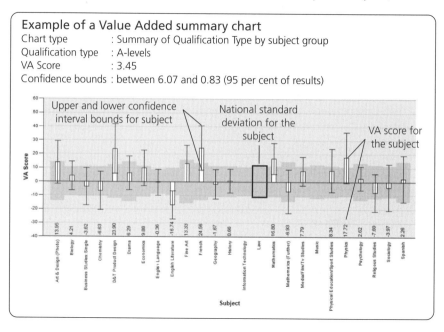

Example of a Value Added summary chart

Chart type   : Summary of Qualification Type by subject group
Qualification type   : A-levels
VA Score   : 3.45
Confidence bounds : between 6.07 and 0.83 (95 per cent of results)

Interpreting VA scores

In the example above the VA score is 3.45, which means that, in general, learners taking A-levels with this provider are achieving an average of 3.45 QCA points above that expected of learners with the same prior attainment at a nationally average provider.

If the VA score is positive and the confidence interval is positive then the performance of the provider's learners is confidently higher, on average, than the national average performance of learners with the same range of prior attainment and following the same qualification. Conversely, if the VA score and confidence interval is negative then the performance of the provider's learners is lower, on average, than the national average.

Value Added comparison reports

VA comparison reports and charts show the performance of a provider's learners in a given qualification subject compared to the national performance for that qualification subject, taking into account the prior attainment of the provider's cohort of learners. The ad hoc version of this report also allows users to select subsets of learners.

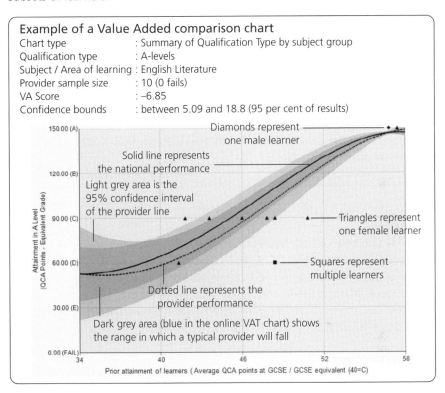

Example of a Value Added comparison chart

Chart type   : Summary of Qualification Type by subject group
Qualification type   : A-levels
Subject / Area of learning : English Literature
Provider sample size   : 10 (0 fails)
VA Score   : −6.85
Confidence bounds   : between 5.09 and 18.8 (95 per cent of results)

Chances reports

The chances report and chart shows the percentage likelihood of learners with given prior attainments achieving a particular grade in a qualification at an institution with results that are in line with the national average.

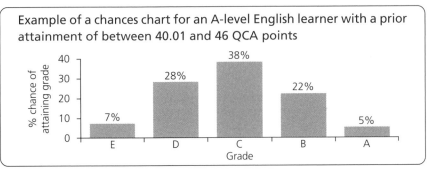

Example of a chances chart for an A-level English learner with a prior attainment of between 40.01 and 46 QCA points

Contextualised Value Added

Another type of learner progress measure is the Achievement and Attainment Tables (AAT) Post-16 Contextualised Value Added (CVA) figures published by the Department for Children, Schools and Families (DCSF). It was piloted in 2007 and rolled out in 2008, with the results available from the DCSF website for each school and college.

CVA is not very different from VA. The basic principle of measuring progress from the end of Key Stage 4 to qualifications attained at Key Stage 5 remains the same. However, CVA measures take account of a number of other explanatory factors which have been observed to impact on its students' results, even after allowing for their prior attainment, such as gender, the type of qualification and size of the learning programme they have studied. CVA therefore gives a much fairer measure of the effectiveness of an institution. This means that comparisons against other schools and colleges are more meaningful.

DCSF website: http://tinyurl.com/yctzv7f

CVA scores
The DCSF publish four CVA figures for each school and college.
- The Key Stage 4 (such as GCSE) to 5 (such as A-level) score
- The upper limit score with a 95% confidence interval
- The lower limit score with a 95% confidence interval
- A coverage indicator, showing the percentage of learner included. Where the coverage is below 50% CVA scores are not published.

CVA percentiles
The CVA percentiles give the distribution of CVA scores and show where institutions are placed nationally compared to other institutions, based on the CVA score.

CVA Score	Percentile
1033.1 – 1102.7	Top 5% of schools and colleges nationally
1014.7 – 1033.1	Next 20% of schools and colleges nationally
1006.2 – 1014.7	Next 15% of schools and colleges nationally
995.6 – 1006.2	Middle 20% of schools and colleges nationally
986.4 – 995.6	Next 15% of schools and colleges nationally
964.1 – 986.4	Next 20% of schools and colleges nationally
918.0 – 964.1	Bottom 5% of schools and colleges nationally

Issues with CVA

The problem with CVA scores is that many have questioned whether it really provides a reliable way to make provider comparisons, and even the DCSF advises caution on its website, saying "it is important these complementary measures are not focussed on in isolation, as to do so could give rise to misleading interpretation of an institution's performance." Ofsted has stated that CVA tables cannot be used to compare one provider with another, saying: "No meaning can be attached to an absolute CVA value, and any ranking of schools by their CVA values is meaningless." (BBC News, 06/08/08, http://tinyurl.com/yjbrd6d)

In fact, there are a number of issues associated with the methodology which suggest the CVA measure should be treated with caution.

CVA Issue	Argument
The CVA does not actually include genuinely contextualising factors.	Neither learner ethnicity nor level of social deprivation is used within the measure.
The CVA data source is incomplete.	Data for CVA analysis is drawn directly from awarding bodies. This means some qualifications, such as AS-level certificates, are excluded when schools and colleges choose not to 'cash-in'. Also, some qualifications that are failed by learners are not reported as 'not yet passed' by the awarding body and therefore excluded from CVA analysis. The CVA data also only includes those learners who complete their two years of study.
The CVA does not differentiate between qualification types.	The CVA methodology treats all A-levels as if they were of equal difficulty, something which VA analysis strongly suggests is not the case (p.68). As a consequence arts and humanities based providers tend to have higher CVA scores than providers that deliver a greater proportion of mathematics and science.
The CVA can disadvantage providers that deliver more qualifications per learner.	The CVA calculation makes an adjustment according to the number of A-levels (or equivalents) taken by the learner. The result of this adjustment can lead to providers delivering a relatively high volume of qualifications per learner receiving a lower CVA score than those providers delivering fewer qualifications per learner.

Framework for Excellence

> The Learner Views Survey is a key element of the FfE. Results will give providers an insight into a broad range of areas such as teaching quality, information on progression and learning support. This feedback should be embraced and taken on board throughout the quality monitoring process.
>
> Shane Chowen, Vice President (Further Education), National Union of Students

Framework for Excellence overview

The core FfE performance indicators

The specific FfE performance indicators

Using the Framework for Excellence

The Framework for Excellence (FfE) is a 'unified post-16 performance assessment tool' which was nationally rolled-out in 2008/09 when eight performance indicators were applied to 1,218 providers. The 2009/10 FfE described here has been simplified, and (subject to further testing and evaluation) will also apply to school sixth forms for 2010/11.

FfE is the Government's annual performance assessment framework for further education colleges and post-16 education and training providers funded by the LSC. It is formed from a set of key performance indicators, covering success rates, the views of learners and employers, learner destinations and finance. Together, these provide an independent, quantitative assessment of the performance of individual providers and the sector as a whole.

It is designed to be useful to:
- employers (who will be able to make better-informed decisions about their choice of provider);
- individual learners, their parents, and potential learners (who will be able to make better-informed decisions about where to go to learn or train);
- commissioners (who will be able to inform their commissioning and performance management decisions);
- providers themselves (who will be able to use the FfE as a diagnostic tool to identify possible weaknesses and to head towards – or maintain – a universally-agreed standard of excellence);
- policy-making bodies (who will get a bigger, clearer picture of the current state of national provision).

Source: *http://ffe.lsc.gov.uk/faq* (December 2009)

The six performance indicators (PIs) in 2009/10 are:
1. learner views (*p.76*)
2. learner destinations (*p.76*)
3. employer views (*p.78*)
4. success rates (*p.77*)
5. financial health (*p.79*)
6. financial management and control (*p.79*)

Funding per successful outcome will not be calculated and is under review (*p.77*).

The FfE has been developed by the LSC on behalf of BIS and DCSF. In April 2010 it became the responsibility of the Skills Funding Agency. The FfE is still in development and, in collaboration with the sector, further changes may be required from 2010/11 and beyond (*p.20*).

Note

At the time of writing there was a dedicated FfE website at http://ffe.lsc.gov.uk. The Framework for Excellence Bulletin can be subscribed to by emailing frameworkfor excellence@lsc.gov.uk and inserting the word 'Bulletin' in the subject header.

Framework for Excellence overview

The Framework for Excellence (FfE) is often referred to as a 'balanced scorecard' with performance indicators within a range of categories. For example, it grades success rates (performance), learner and employer views (responsiveness) as well as finance. For 2009/10 FfE consists of three core (applied to all providers) and three specific (applied only to relevant providers) performance indicators (PIs). A score for each PI is calculated to establish a grade, and some grades and scores are published. At present, the intention is not to produce an overall performance rating for 2010 or 2011, although the need for a summary rating is being kept under review.

Framework for Excellence performance indicators for 2009/10

Source: *Framework for Excellence Provider Guide*, LSC (September 2009)

Category	Seven indicators	Core or specific	Published or unpublished
Learner and qualification success	Success rates	Core	Published
Learner views	Learner views	Core	Published
Learner destinations	Learner destinations	Core	Published
Responsiveness to employers	Employer views	Specific	Published
	Amount of training (not graded)	Specific	Published
	Training quality standard (TQS)	Specific	Published
Financial health and management	Financial health	Specific	Unpublished
	Financial management and control evaluation	Specific	Unpublished

Exemptions from the Framework for 2009/10 include:

- sixth-form schools (inclusion is planned for 2010/11, subject to piloting);
- universities or higher education provision in colleges funded by the Higher Education Funding Council for England (HEFCE);
- learners aged 14 and 15 who are in colleges;
- organisations only delivering European Social Fund (ESF), University for Industry (Ufi) or Informal Adult Learning (IAL) provision;
- Offender Learning and Skills Service (OLASS) provision;
- provision funded by other government department or agencies.

For in-scope providers, the majority of the courses used to calculate most of the FfE performance indicators relates to learner- and employer-responsive provision. Also, there is no longer a £30,000 minimum amount of funding that a provider needs to receive before they are included.

Provider dissemination

All the relevant scores and grades, and other supporting information for each performance indicator, are made available to individual providers (planned for spring 2010). These can be accessed from the FfE application on the password-protected Provider Gateway website. As well as individual provider results, high-level benchmarking and, over time, trend data will be published as well as individual provider results. Providers can use these to inform their quality improvement plans and judgments within their self-assessment reports (p. 98).

Publication

A public reporting website is also being developed to be launched in June 2010. This will include the FfE outputs for each provider alongside their latest Ofsted Overall Effectiveness grade and a link to their inspection report. This will be the first time that FfE grades will have been published for individual providers. At the time of writing, the final detail regarding the output and dissemination process was subject to ongoing consultation with national stakeholders and provider representative bodies.

Note

The FfE website will include a web address for each provider. This information is sourced from the UKRLP database (p. 109). Therefore, providers should log in to the UKRLP to review and update their information where necessary, and most importantly to tick the box which allows the FfE website to publish their web address.

The future for FfE

FfE will continue to be developed as improvements are made, and the range of providers and performance measures are refined. The LSC has said: "We know we need to refine some of the existing PIs further. We will work collaboratively with the sector and continue to ask providers, their representative organisations and other stakeholders for their views on this." (Framework for Excellence: Improvements made for 2009/10 as a result of implementation in 2008/09, LSC, November 2009)

What seems clear is that in the coming years FfE will become an increasingly important performance assessment tool. In particular, it will be a key tool used to form judgements about providers for the purpose of commissioning or decommissioning provision (p. 60).

The core FfE performance indicators

Learner views (published)

The learner views performance indicator is calculated from the results of a short web-based survey consisting of nine main questions. The surveys must be administered by the provider, with a minimum number of responses required dependent on the overall number of learners. The survey applies to all learner- or employer-responsive funded learners.

Proposed learner views assessment criteria (PI 1)	
Grade	Score
Outstanding	90% or greater
Good	80% to less than 90%
Satisfactory	70% to less than 80%
Inadequate	Less than 70%

Learner destinations (published)

For FfE 2009/10 the destinations collected are for 16–18-year-olds and adult priority learners who completed a funded programme in 2007/08 and progressed to one or more of the following destinations in 2008/09:

- enrolled at the same or higher level than in 2007/08;
- remained in employment, with improved job security or career prospects;
- entered employment or training, having previously been unemployed.

In some cases learners will be matched between 2007/08 and 2008/09 ILR and HE data files to determine progression. In other cases, such as to determine progression to employment, contractors will telephone all eligible leavers. A significant number of learners could not be contacted for the 2008/09 FfE as the ILR field for the learner telephone number (L23) was missing, incorrect or incomplete. Providers are therefore encouraged to ensure all learner contact details are updated regularly and are as accurate, and complete, as possible at the end of their course.

Proposed learner destinations assessment criteria (PI 2)	
Grade	Score
Outstanding	85% or greater
Good	72.5% to less than 85%
Satisfactory	60% to less than 72.5%
Inadequate	Less than 60%%

If quality thresholds are not met (for example less than 30 destinations are established) then a grade will not be given.

Learner and qualification success (published)

The success rate measure is a score obtained by combining the learner-responsive (LR) and employer-responsive (ER) success rates for several qualification types:

- LR long qualifications (excluding A-levels, AS and A2);
- LR short and very short qualifications;
- A-levels (including AS and A2);
- Apprenticeships (Level 2) and Advanced Apprenticeships (Level 3);
- Train to Gain full Level 2 and full Level 3 qualifications.

The resulting score is supplemented where relevant with information from the Learner Achievement Tracker (LAT) A-level value added (*p.66*).

Success rates assessment criteria (PI 4)
As at March 2010 the scoring and grading criteria had yet to be confirmed.

Funding per successful outcome (under review)

The concept of this performance indicator applies to the demand-led funding and success rate methodology to 2008/09 data to determine the average amount of funding that the provider received for each successful outcome. Before aggregating across 16–18 and 19+ learner- and employer-responsive funding models to determine the overall provider average, it is adjusted by:

- a programme weighting and disadvantage factor to represent the additional resources that a provider uses;
- an age factor to represent the different funding regimes for those aged over 18.

Proposed funding per successful outcome assessment criteria	
Grade	Score
Outstanding	80 or greater
Good	50 to less than 80
Satisfactory	15 to less than 50
Inadequate	Less than 15

Once the total average 'adjusted and weighted nominal funding rate' has been calculated, this is compared to a table of rates to determine the score.

Note
Due to changes in the funding methodology and the application of FfE to schools with sixth forms, this PI is under review and will not be calculated for 2009/10.

The specific FfE performance indicators

Employer views (published)

Employer data is gathered by the Skills Funding Agency from the providers' Individualised Learner Record (ILR) for 2008/09. Employers are then contacted directly by Skills Funding Agency contractors to invite them to complete an online, email or paper-based questionnaire, or an automated telephone response survey. Providers themselves are key to the success of the survey by encouraging the employers that they work with to take part. Only the first response from each employer will be used to calculate a score. The aggregate score is between 0 and 10 and the scores from all employers and for all questions carry an equal weighting.

Proposed employer views assessment criteria (PI 3)	
Grade	Score
Outstanding	9 or greater (or see TQS below)
Good	8 to less than 9
Satisfactory	6 to less than 8
Inadequate	Less than 6

Providers who wholly train their own employees or whose allocation for employer-responsive funding is less than £30,000 are exempt from the employer views survey.

The Training Quality Standard (published)

The Training Quality Standard (TQS) is an independently assessed standard for employer responsiveness that was launched in May 2008. Part A of the TQS focuses on responsiveness, and providers that are certified to Part A for their whole organisation on or before 23 March 2010 will automatically be given an 'outstanding' grade for employer views. For more information about the TQS visit www.trainingqualitystandard.co.uk

Proposed TQS assessment criteria (PI 3)	
Grade	Score
Outstanding	TQS Part A before 23/03/10
Determined by questionnaire (see below)	No TQS Part A before 23/03/10

Amount of training (not graded) (published)

The volume of employer-responsive provision, such as Train to Gain and Apprenticeship learners and funding, will be published alongside a provider's other employer-responsive indicators. This is to aid those interested in understanding the scale of a provider's employer-responsive provision.

Financial health (unpublished)

For colleges, the financial health score for the 2009/10 FfE is derived from the financial record for the year ending 31 July 2009. For non-college providers it is the latest full accounts or equivalent. This performance indicator is also used in the financial intervention strategy (p.60).

It consists of three elements, each of which can score up to 100 points.
1. Current ratio (solvency)
2. Operating surplus or deficit as a percentage of turnover/income (sustainability)
3. Borrowing as a percentage of certain reserves and debt (status).

Scores for all three elements are added together and an additional 50 or 100 points can be earned in recognition of consistency. Therefore providers can achieve a maximum of 400 points.

Proposed financial health assessment criteria (PI 5)	
Grade	Score
Outstanding	310–400 points
Good	220–300 points
Satisfactory	120–210 points
Inadequate	110 or less points

Some providers, such as NHS trusts and companies with LSC contracts of no more than five percent of annual turnover, are exempt from this indicator, as are providers who receive less than £50,000 of funding a year.

Financial management and control evaluation (unpublished)

Providers annually complete a Financial Management and Control Evaluation (FMCE) template. For the 2009/10 FfE this is based on the period 1 August 2008 to 31 July 2009. The FMCE includes a series of questions concerning accountability, financial planning, internal control and financial monitoring. Providers must answer the questions and self-assess the application of one of the four FfE grades. This then forms part of the overall self-assessment grade for financial management.

Proposed FMCE assessment criteria (PI 6)
Self-assessed by providers, but audit teams will initially complete a desk-based review. Full validation will normally be included as part of planned audit visits.

Non-college providers that receive less than £50,000 annually of in-scope government funding do not have to complete an FMCE.

Using the Framework for Excellence

The Framework for Excellence (FfE) scores and grades will be used by a range of organisations and individuals, some of whom are mentioned here.

Colleges and training providers
Providers should be using FfE to self-assess performance (*p.98*).

> The Framework should be used by colleges and providers to assess and improve their own performance, and incorporate the findings of self assessment into reports for governing bodies and boards. The LSC expects all providers in scope to use the Framework's scores as part of the evidence for self-assessment reports submitted to the LSC.
>
> Source: *FfE, An Introductory Guide for College Governors*, LSC (May 2009)

Learners and employers

> The new performance measures will mean that every prospective student and employer wanting to access further education will be able to see the quality and responsiveness they can expect from an institution.
>
> Source: *FfE Launch Press Release*, Bill Rammell, DIUS (June 2008)

The Learning and Skills Improvement Service (LSIS)
FfE will help LSIS identify colleges eligible for support (*p.111*).

Ofsted
The Office for Standards in Education (Ofsted) plan to use FfE extensively. As the statement below says, not only will Ofsted use FfE to inform its judgements, it will also use it to determine how often to inspect.

> When a full set of FfE performance indicators are published, Ofsted plans to use them: to inform the scheduling of inspections; as contributory evidence to inform inspection judgements and; to support the issuing of 'interim assessments' in the form of a letter.
>
> Source: *FfE website*, LSC, http://ffe.lsc.gov.uk/faq (December 2009)

Commissioners
The 2009/10 FfE grades will be used by the Skills Funding Agency to commission adult provision. It will also be of particular interest to local authorities, as they will use it to commission 16–19 provision for 2011/12.

> Local authorities, who will be separately commissioning 16–19 provision from colleges and other training institutions according to the National Commissioning Framework, will use the Framework for Excellence to support the commissioning of high quality learning places.
>
> Source: *Skills for Growth, Skills Strategy*, BIS (November 2009)

Beyond 2009/10

At present the Government is looking at ways to use FfE for additional purposes, such as to give providers rated 'outstanding' enhanced freedoms across their total budget.

The FfE structure, methodologies and method of publication are kept under review, and will change to some extent, not least to accommodate school sixth form provision in 2011/12. Perhaps the most radical change proposed is the adoption of a traffic light system, similar to food labelling.

Drawing on the Framework for Excellence data, all training will be covered by public 'traffic light' information, providing quality assured data about performance at course and institutional level.

A model proposed by the UK Commission for Employment and Skills (UKCES) to illustrate how the new information might be presented is shown below. However, we are not committed at this stage to a particular model; we expect it to evolve in the context of an overall approach to the performance assessment of post-16 providers that is appropriately aligned with the single report card being developed to measure schools' performance.

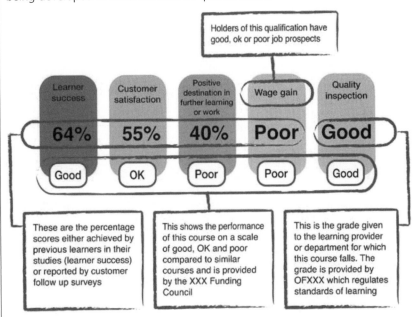

We will look to provide data through the 'traffic light' system down to course level wherever possible. We will want closer involvement from the sector in determining the standards that are set and in collecting and publishing data.

Source: *Skills for Growth, Skills Strategy*, BIS (November 2009)

Data quality

Getting the data right is critical; at a recent Foundation Learning Champions' conference, putting in place effective data systems was identified as one of the top ten actions in an effective implementation plan.

Jane Moore, Head of Skills for Life, Fareham College

Data accuracy, validity and good practice

Data credibility and quality assessment reports

The success rate data credibility issue

Data audit and comparison tools

Data quality is not only important, it is a prerequisite in post-16 education and training. This is because enrolment and learner data, in the form of the Individualised Learning Record (ILR), is used to determine both funding levels and a range of performance judgments (p.22).

The information authority is working hard to help providers improve the quality of their data. It has categorised data quality by a series of dimensions.

Dimensions of data quality	
Dimension	**Principles**
Accuracy	In most cases data should represent what actually happened. However, in some cases, such as for success rates, the data recorded is based only on what was planned (p.89).
Completeness	Data should not contain invalid or missing data. This includes avoiding the use of codes for unknowns, wherever possible (p.87).
Validity and credibility	Data should be recorded and maintained in compliance with the relevant rules and definitions (p.84).
Reliability and consistency	Data should be collected and processed consistently.
Timeliness	Data collection should be captured and returned as quickly as necessary to support processes for which it is collected (p.28)
Relevance	Where data is captured in addition to that which is contractually required, it should be relevant to the purpose for which it is used.

Source: Modelled on the *Data Quality Framework, the information authority* (January 2010)

Some providers will regularly measure how good they are at data quality based on dimensions such as these. This helps them quickly resolve any issues and improve practices going forward. It can also be helpful to document data-related processes, as staff will often have very detailed knowledge which would otherwise be lost when they move on. This chapter contains links to a series of data-related good practice documents (p.85).

This chapter also takes a closer look at some of the tools and reports which are available to providers to help identify data which may be inaccurate or incomplete. A number of these are relatively new and are subject to change. For example, at the time of writing the plan was to include the data credibility reports (p.86) that are currently accessible from the online data collections system, within the Learner Information Suite (LIS) (p.42).

Data accuracy, validity and good practice

Accurate data capture in post-16 education is critically important, not least because learner- and employer-responsive Individualised Learner Record (ILR) data (p.22) is used to calculate funding values and measure performance. Implications of inaccurate ILR data capture include:

- management decisions being based on false evidence;
- risk of funding claw-back and ability to gain future contracts;
- unsatisfactory Ofsted inspection judgements (p.89);
- government targets, and thus policies, based on false evidence.

Provider ILR data must conform to the rules within the ILR specification (p.24), which is published by the information authority (p.106). If the ILR contains even one error it should not be returned for funding purposes.

ILR validation reports

There are a number of tools which are available to help providers identify inaccurate or duplicate ILR data (p.90). The most important of these is the Learner Information Suite (LIS), which validates ILR data against the national specification (p.42).

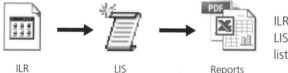

ILR   LIS   Reports

ILR files are imported into the LIS, and rule violation reports list errors and warnings.

The LIS validation reports are used before making ILR returns. However, it should be remembered that ILR data that has been validated by the LIS does not necessarily mean it is accurate, nor credible (p.88).

Rule Violations Summary (Full Validation)

Provider : MADEUP COLLEGE (100000)
UKPRN : 10000000
ILR File : A10000000000000000000.W06

Year : 2009/10
Collection : W06

Filters: Funding Rule: (All)
    Warning: (All)

Summary Report

Total Learner Count :	1468		Number of Learners with Warnings Only :	540
Fully Validated Learners :			Total Data Records :	2865
Number of Valid :	1402		Number of Files Imported :	1
Number of Invalid :	66		Footer Count :	2867
Funding Rule Only Learners :			Duplicate Record Count :	0
Number of Valid :	1460			
Number of Invalid :	6		Duplicate Learner Count :	0
Total Aims Count :	1693		Employer Responsive Provision :	1589
ASL Funded Aims :	0		of which Programme Aims :	214
16-18 Learner Responsive Aims :	0		Non-LSC Funded Aims :	8
Adult Learner Responsive Aims :	0		Other LSC Funded Aims :	95
ESF Co-Financed Aims :	0			

Please note that the web portal applies additional validation rules. The LIS column on the ILR Validation Rules spreadsheet shows if a rule is applied by LIS.

ILR good practice case studies

There are a number of ILR good practice case studies on *the information authority* website, including one written about collecting unique learner numbers (*p.108*). Below are suggestions from the South Devon College data quality case study. Visit: http://tinyurl.com/yedfjnh

- Set up a routine to regularly clean and report on ILR data
- Look at methods to effectively report this data to Senior Managers within your institution. These could include:
  - A weekly emailed funding summary, including underlying data at course and learner level to enable investigation
  - Access to a web-based reporting system, available to all staff, showing all learner and course data

Data health checks and organisation information

A particularly useful good practice guide, written by Jane Owen and Jeff Alterman, was published by the Learning and Skills Development Agency in 2003. The guide, which remains relevant today, includes: data health check templates; advice on target-setting processes; advice on information policies and data audits as well as emphasising the importance of organisation information, as opposed to simply management information. *Hitting the target: target setting and information systems for the learning and skills sector* is available free of change from: http://tinyurl.com/y948hzd

Using data to drive up the quality of teaching and learning

In September 2008 Ofsted published *How colleges improve, a review of effective practice*. This includes a number of examples of how colleges have used data to support the quality improvement agenda, such as "establishing a centralised system so that teachers had confidence in the data". The Ofsted report is available from: http://tinyurl.com/ybmaxrv

Data handling and security

Becta, the government IT agency 'leading the national drive to ensure the effective and innovative use of technology throughout learning', has produced a series of guides on how to handle and secure sensitive and personal data on learners, staff and other individuals. These guides can be accessed from: http://tinyurl.com/yjg9ab4

Data Protection

It is critical that all providers and other stakeholders ensure that personal data is managed fairly and lawfully, and an individuals' privacy rights are safeguarded. The LSC published information regarding data protection, which includes signposting to other sources of guidance. For example, it includes information about the Data Protection Act and the Information Commissioner's Office (www.ico.gov.uk). Organisations should therefore seek independent advice, where it is required. The LSC document can be accessed from: http://tinyurl.com/yhqxobn

Data credibility and quality assessment reports

Data credibility and quality assessment reports are part of a suite of complementary products, including the Learner Information Suite (*p.42*) and the Data Self-Assessment Tool (*p.90*), designed to help providers improve and maintain the quality of their Individualised Learner Record (ILR) data (*p.22*).

Data credibility reports

Once a provider has made an ILR return they can download a credibility report from the online data collections system (*p.28*). The credibility reports provide summaries of the submitted data, along with key summaries of derived variables calculated on the data by the Data Service. As shown in the image below, the credibility reports also include red, amber and green (RAG) colour-coding on key fields to indicate the completeness of these fields based on *information authority* data standards within the ILR 2009/10 specification, Appendix P (*p.24*).

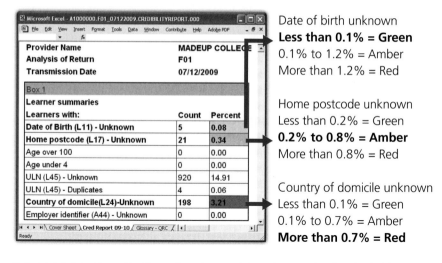

Date of birth unknown
Less than 0.1% = Green
0.1% to 1.2% = Amber
More than 1.2% = Red

Home postcode unknown
Less than 0.2% = Green
0.2% to 0.8% = Amber
More than 0.8% = Red

Country of domicile unknown
Less than 0.1% = Green
0.1% to 0.7% = Amber
More than 0.7% = Red

Cells highlighted in red indicate that the provider's data quality for the field is below the standard expected of in-year returns. Amber cells indicate that it is below the standard expected of end-of-year returns. Green cells indicate the standard has been achieved for in-year and end-of-year returns.

> ### Note
>
> The employer-responsive credibility report also includes a worksheet with length of stay numbers (such as how many have been on the programme more than 48 months). This is for information only, and does not apply credibility standards. Helpfully it also lists the volume of those on-programme beyond the planned end date, early achievers and the number of learners who withdrew within the first six weeks.

Standard data quality assessments

Quality assessment reports present the aggregate results of completeness checks on selected fields against data standards for providers published in the ILR 2009/10 specification, Appendix P (*p.24*).

Information included in ILR quality assessments:

- data standards, where applicable, for in-year and year-end returns;
- null entries;
- average completion rate for selected fields;
- frequency and percentage count of learners or enrolments below data standard for the field;
- frequency and percentage count of providers failing to achieve data standards for the field.

Standard data quality assessments are published on the Data Service website shortly after each learner- and employer-responsive data return.

As shown below, many providers need to improve the collection of prior attainment (*p.25*) and the unique learner numbers (*p.108*).

Standard data quality assessment (2009/10 LR F01)			
ILR field	**Condition**	**Data standard**	**Actual unknown**
Prior attainment	Full Level 2 enrolments	5% or less unknown	21% (62k enrolments)
Prior attainment	Full Level 3 enrolments	3% or less unknown	15% (69k enrolments)
Unique Learner Number	All learners	None set	25% (507k learners)

Standard data quality assessment (2009/10 ER W06)			
ILR field	**Condition**	**Data standard**	**Actual unknown**
Prior attainment	Full Level 2 enrolments	7% or less unknown	2% (16k enrolments)
Prior attainment	Full Level 3 enrolments	5% or less unknown	3% (8k enrolments)
Unique Learner Number	All learners	None set	32% (367k learners)

Success rate data credibility

Success rates have consistently exceeded national targets and increased, on average, by three percentage points each year since 1997. This year-on-year increase is shown in the graph below:

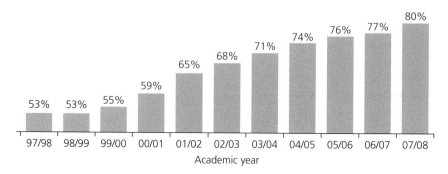

Source: *DfES evidence to Foster Review of FE, and Statistical First Releases (p.18)*

The reasons for success rate rises are often complex, and can, for example, be a combination of:
*   improving the quality and/or quantity of teaching and learning;
*   increasing the quality and/or quantity of additional support;
*   improving the standard of materials and/or the learning environment;
*   qualifications being modularised (such as A-levels in 2002/03);
*   more learners enrolling on less challenging or lower level qualifications;
*   increasingly the learner selection assessment thresholds;
*   any reduction in the standard of qualification assessments;
*   relatively low success rate provision being reduced or cut *(p.60)*;
*   relatively high success rate provision being increased.

Attention has also turned to the way that data is recorded. For example, when providers pay more attention to their data, such as ensuring there are no completed learners with unknown outcomes, this can increase success rates. The message below from Ofsted is also clear, that providers can improve their inspection grades with better data management.

> In one college, the leap from good to outstanding was not made entirely through improving teaching and learning – much was due to managing the data more effectively.
>
> Source: *How colleges improve, a review of effective practice*, Ofsted (September 2008)

However, more recently there has been a concern that some providers have inappropriately exploited the benefits of data management. Knowingly or otherwise, the suggestion is that some providers have been recording data inappropriately and inconsistently, resulting in success rate inflation.

Success rate fact-finding review

The LSC and Ofsted commissioned a success rate fact-finding review, which was published in September 2009. Seven colleges were selected and visited, where a very small number of qualifications undertaken by 16–18-year-old learners were audited. The report concluded that some of the practices identified at the fact-finding visits have led to an artificial increase in success rates. It also said that the guidance is not always clear and interpretations differ between colleges.

Particular issues identified in the review included:
- different practices relating to the recording of 'unfunded' learners;
- the failure to record all learning aims being undertaken by learners;
- changes to planned end dates;
- late changes to a learner's programme of learning;
- inappropriate use of the transfer code.

LSC letter to colleges

As a consequence of the review, the LSC wrote to all providers concerning the "inconsistent and sometimes inappropriate reporting". In particular, the letter to colleges emphasised that:
- there must be a learner record for every learner;
- once a learner is recorded as LSC funded, this must not be changed;
- the learning planned end date should not be changed;
- where an enrolment is recorded as transferred, there must be a corresponding enrolment to which the learner has transferred.

Ofsted letter to colleges

Ofsted has also sent a letter to providers, stating that they will be putting in place the same tests on data that informed the visits to the seven colleges. Where credibility issues are identified, possible outcomes include:
- concluding for some aspects of the college's work that data are unreliable. In this case it may be possible to recalculate some success rates based on data returned before it was finalised;
- concluding that data at the aggregate level are unreliable and looking closely at the data for those qualification aims which curriculum inspectors deem to be representative of their curriculum areas;
- concluding that data in general are unreliable and not placing importance on success rate evidence;
- where data are unreliable, assessing the impact on the overall judgements and grade for leadership and management (p.97).

Tightening up the guidance and removing ambiguity

The LSC's letter acknowledged the need to tighten up the guidance. This work is being led by the information authority (p.106), which is consulting providers and stakeholders. For outstanding queries email servicedesk@thedataservice.org.uk or call 0870 2670001.

Data audit and comparison tools

The Data Self-Assessment Toolkit (DSAT)

The DSAT (also referred to as Provider DSAT or PDSAT) is a tool which should be used to help identify problems with data, such as credibility. It is available free of charge to providers, and can be used for both learner- and employer-responsive data.

There is in fact an expectation from the funding body that providers will regularly use the DSAT (such as once per month), and data auditors will often use the tool themselves to identify potential data credibility issues.

> To assist in making good-quality Individualised Learner Record and funding returns to the LSC, providers should make use of the DSAT reports that are relevant to their own provision and data.
>
> Source: *LSC Funding Guidance 2008/09*, LSC (September 2008)

The DSAT reports

To produce DSAT reports, the Individualised Learner Record (ILR) file (*p.22*) needs to be imported into the Learner Information Suite (LIS) software (*p.42*), which then produces an ILR database (DB) file. The ILR DB along with the latest Learning Aim Database (LAD) (*p.32*) is then imported into the DSAT software.

Example data-flow for producing DSAT reports:

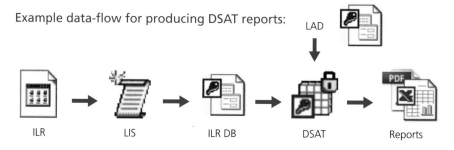

| ILR | LIS | ILR DB | DSAT | Reports |

The DSAT restrictions

Providers are reminded that DSAT reports are simply a guide to where further investigation is required, as explained within the DSAT user guide:

> The DSAT does not produce definitive results within its reports. The tool is designed to provide users with indicative reports that are based on areas of concern and risk that may require further investigation for clarification and rectification purposes. However, DSAT can assist providers in verifying and checking their ILR data for validity and correctness in certain areas. The LIS and other tools provided by the LSC should be used to provide definitive results in all areas.
>
> Source: *DSAT v.10.00 User Guide*, LSC (December 2009)

Achievement and Data Management (ADaM) tool

In direct response to the success rate data credibility issue outlined on page 88, I have worked with Drake Lane Associates to create a support tool. ADaM, which works for both learner- and employer-responsive provision, highlights where data has been changed. It works by importing two different Individualised Learner Record (ILR) files within the same year, such as F04 and F05, or W12 and W13 (p.29), and produces comparison reports. It works for 2007/08, 2008/09 and 2009/10 ILRs.

Example data-flow for producing ADaM comparison reports:

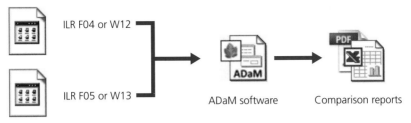

ILR F04 or W12

ILR F05 or W13

ADaM software

Comparison reports

ADaM ILR data comparison reports

ADaM has been designed to produce reports highlighting the issues which may impact on success rates, such as those identified within the LSC letter (p.89). Therefore, ADaM reports highlight:

- enrolments where the funding source has changed;
- enrolments which have been removed (no longer exist in the ILR);
- changes to planned end dates;
- issues associated with transfers, such as the status being changed from a withdrawal to a transfer, a transfer to a lower level and transfers not appearing to have a subsequent new enrolment.

Key benefits of ADaM to providers

- Areas of potential concern can be assessed and investigated internally prior to them being raised by auditors or inspectors.
- Pre-emptive analyses will provide time to build cases in defence of data management practices where appropriate.
- Poor data management practices (in LSC and Ofsted terms) can be highlighted and remedial action taken where appropriate.
- Potential reductions in inspection grades may be averted (p.89).
- Reports are in PDF format with additional MS Excel and Access export options, allowing for linking to provider systems for bespoke analysis.
- In addition to the reports aligned to the issues highlighted within the LSC letter, providers can also compare other ILR data fields.

To find out more, and purchase ADaM, visit:
www.drakelane.co.uk/adam

Inspection and self-assessment

> Embedding self assessment report work into staff one-to-one monthly sessions can reduce end of year SAR stress and raise the overall quality.
>
> Mia Wylie, Contracts and Information Manager, ELATT

Ofsted inspection overview

Full inspection reports and grades

Self-assessment reports

Improving self-assessment

Ofsted is the Office for Standards in Education, Children's Services and Skills, and it regulates and inspects education and skills for learners of all ages (p.111). In addition to schools, Ofsted inspects colleges, private training providers, local authorities and other providers who receive public funding to deliver provision as part of the further education and skills sector. In the main, the provision it is inspecting within the further education and skills sector has been funded from either the learner- or employer-responsive funding model.

Purpose of inspection

The overall aim of inspection is to evaluate the efficiency and effectiveness of the provision of education and training in meeting the needs of learners.

Inspection arrangements, together with other government initiatives, are intended to accelerate the pace of quality improvement in the further education and skills sector.

The main purposes of inspections are to:
- provide users with information; this informs their choices and preferences about the effectiveness of the providers they use or may use in the future
- help bring about improvement by identifying strengths and areas for improvement, highlighting good practice and judging what steps need to be taken to improve provision further
- provide the relevant Secretaries of State and other stakeholders with an independent public account of the quality of education and training, the standards achieved and the efficiency with which resources are managed
- make judgements that may inform Comprehensive Area Assessments in each local area.

Source: *Handbook for the inspection of FE and skills*, Ofsted (January 2010)

Inspection is a critical performance regime, the judgements within which draw heavily on qualitative evidence (such as lesson observations) as well as quantitative evidence (such as success rates). The published judgements and grades (p.95) are used to inform not only the public, but also to support commissioning decisions, share and raise best practice, and in a small minority of cases they lead to external intervention.

However, quality assurance is much more than just an inspection from Ofsted. Inspection is part of a much broader approach to improving the quality of the provision and outcomes for learners. The best providers will follow a well established cycle of action planning, which includes the setting and monitoring of an appropriate range of challenging yet achievable targets. In particular, all providers have to submit an annual self-assessment report (p.98).

Ofsted inspection overview

Ofsted operates a variety of inspections, which are proportionate to the risk and selected according to the performance level of the provider. Reports are published online (p.111) and providers are normally given two to three working weeks' notice before any of the following inspection types:

Type	Frequency	Purpose
Full inspection	Every four years, or up to six years for high-performing providers. New providers will be inspected between year one and year four.	Inspection visit to grade provider against Common Inspection Framework 2009.
Interim assessment	Within three years of last full inspection.	Desk-based review, summarised in a letter.
Focused monitoring visit	Normally within two years of a full inspection for providers judged as satisfactory for overall effectiveness and satisfactory or inadequate for capacity to improve.	To monitor progress according to areas identified during inspections and/or inspect new areas of work, such as Train to Gain.
Subject or survey visit	Survey inspection visits take place at a selected number of providers, including those judged as outstanding, each year.	To explore specific aspects of work, on topics linked to national priorities.
Providers that are judged to be inadequate for overall effectiveness or for an aspect or subject will have a reinspection monitoring visit.		
Reinspection monitoring visit	Six to eight months after last full inspection.	To inspect themes identified through the previous inspection.
Following a reinspection providers will either have:		
a) Partial reinspection	12 to 15 months after most recent full inspection where there is an inadequate grade for an aspect or subject area.	To inspect and grade relevant areas and focus on a provider's capacity to improve.
b) Full reinspection	12 to 15 months after most recent full inspection where there is an inadequate grade for overall effectiveness.	To inspect all aspects of a provider's provision against the Common Inspection Framework 2009.

Common inspection framework 2009

The *Common inspection framework for further education and skills 2009* is based on the 'common evaluation schedule', which informs all of Ofsted's inspections and sets out the judgements inspectors will make. It is at the heart of the inspection as it sets out the structure of the inspection and identifies the key aspects against which judgements will be made.

The common inspection framework (CIF) lists questions that inspectors must ask of every provider of education, training and development. These questions are structured around areas which are then graded. The diagram below shows the grading structure.

Structure of Ofsted inspection grades
Source: *Common inspection framework for FE and skills 2009*, Ofsted (2009)

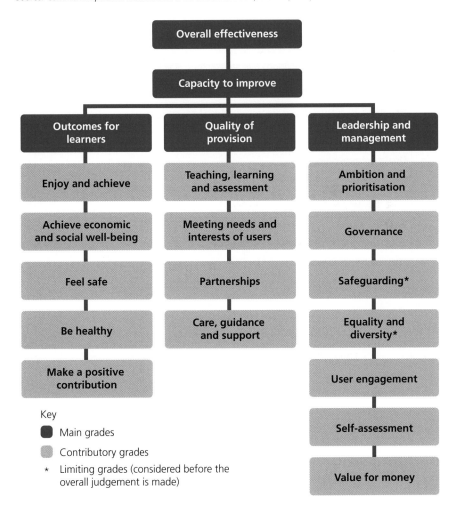

Full inspection reports and grades

Typically, within 25 days of the inspection the report or letter is published on the Ofsted website (www.ofsted.gov.uk). Full inspection reports are structured as follows:

Information about the provider

Inspection reports begin with an overview of the provider, including information about the relevant geographical area, types of programmes delivered, type and volume of learners engaged and any partnerships with other providers.

Summary report

The report then lists the main grades and limiting grades. Grades are also listed for any subject areas for which curriculum specialists observed lessons. Below is an example of how summary grades are reported.

Summary report

Grades: 1 is outstanding; 2 is good; 3 is satisfactory; 4 is inadequate

Overall effectiveness of provision	Grade 2
Capacity to improve	Grade 2

	Grade
Outcomes for learners	2
Quality of provision	2
Leadership and management	2
Safeguarding	2
Equality and diversity	2

Subject areas	
Engineering and manufacturing technologies	3
Literacy and Numeracy	2

Overall effectiveness

In this section a number of paragraphs summarise overall effectiveness, such as: "This is a good college with a good capacity to improve."

Main findings

This is a more detailed section that outlines the main findings, such as: "There is a strong commitment to equality and diversity from senior leaders."

What the provider needs to do to improve

This section includes statements about issues which require improvement, such as: "Ensure that timeframes for completion are appropriate for individual learners."

Summary of learner and employer views

This section lists examples of 'what learners and employers like', and 'what they would like to see improved'.

Main inspection report and subject areas

These sections provide a commentary and judgements for the main grades, as well as any subject areas that had been graded separately.

Record of Main Findings (RMF)

The final page lists all the grades for the relevant provision types.

Record of Main Findings (RMF)

Madeup College

Learning types: **14 – 16:** Young apprenticeships; Diplomas; **16-18 Learner responsive:** FE full- and part-time courses, Foundation learning tier, including Entry to Employment; **19+ responsive:** FE full- and part-time courses; **Employer responsive:** Train to Gain, apprenticeships

Grades using the 4 point scale 1: Outstanding; 2: Good; 3: Satisfactory; 4: Inadequate	Overall	14-16	16-18 Learner responsive	19+ Learner responsive	Employer responsive
Approximate number of enrolled learners Full-time learners	4,113	334	1,394	1,547	1,544
Overall effectiveness	2	3	2	2	2
Capacity to improve	2				
Outcomes for learners	2	3	2	2	2
How well do learners achieve and enjoy their learning?	2				
How well do learners attain their learning goals?	3				
How well do learners progress?	2				
How well do learners improve their economic and social well-being through learning and development?	2				
How safe do learners feel?	2				
Are learners able to make informed choices about their own health and well being?*	2				
How well do learners make a positive contribution to the community?*	3				
Quality of provision	2	2	2	2	2
How effectively do teaching, training and assessment support learning and development?	1				
How effectively does the provision meet the needs and interests of users?	2				
How well partnerships with schools, employers, community groups and others lead to benefits for learners?	1				
How effective are the care, guidance and support learners receive in helping them to achieve?	2				
Leadership and management	2	2	2	2	2
How effectively do leaders and managers raise expectations and promote ambition throughout the organisation?	3				
How effectively do governors and supervisory bodies provide leadership, direction and challenge?*	2				
How effectively does the provider promote the safeguarding of learners?	2				
How effectively does the provider actively promote equality and diversity, tackle discrimination and narrow the achievement gap?	2				
How effectively does the provider engage with users to support and promote improvement?	3				
How effectively does self-assessment improve the quality of the provision and outcomes for learners?	2				
How efficiently and effectively does the provider use its available resources to secure value for money?	2				

*where applicable to the type of provision

Self-assessment reports

As part of the inspection of leadership and management, inspectors judge and comment on how effectively performance is monitored, evaluated and improved through quality assurance and self-assessment. As such, providers are required to publish an annual self-assessment report (SAR), which is uploaded to the online Provider Gateway (p.15).

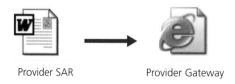

Provider SAR   Provider Gateway

Once published online, the SAR is available to:
- Ofsted
- Skills Funding Agency
- Local Authorities

The format of the SAR tends to mirror that of an inspection report (p.96), and includes grades. During the inspection, Ofsted will then use the SAR to judge and comment on the provider's ability to appraise themselves honestly for strengths, areas for improvement and how well self-assessment is integrated into an overall quality improvement strategy.

The effectiveness of self-assessment is a contributory grade within full inspection reports, supporting the Leadership and Management main grade (p.95). The inspection handbook outlines how it is evaluated:

How effectively does self-assessment improve the quality of the provision and outcomes for learners?

To make their judgement, inspectors will evaluate the extent to which:
- the provider has effective processes for monitoring and evaluating performance and tackling weaknesses;
- the analysis of data on performance and progress is used to improve performance;
- action plans have clear, ambitious and realistic targets that show provision will be developed for learners and are implemented and monitored effectively.

Inspectors will take into account, where relevant:
- the thoroughness and accuracy of the provider's self-assessment process and report
- the use of self-assessment as part of a continuous cycle of review and evaluation of the provider's performance against challenging targets that lead to sustained quality improvement
- the involvement of all staff, including partner providers
- the use of a range of analysis as evidence (p.99)
- how self-assessment outcomes produce realistic action plans.

Source: *Handbook for the inspection of FE and skills*, Ofsted (January 2010)

Using data and targets in self-assessment

In post-16 education and training there is a wealth of data recorded about the learner and their enrolments within both the Individualised Learner Record (p.22) and elsewhere (such as attendance and punctuality). In the context of quality assurance, a range of these should be used appropriately to identify both strengths and areas for improvement. Most importantly, this data should be used within the self-assessment report to set and monitor challenging yet attainable targets.

Examples of data used to set targets and evidence judgements:
*   retention, achievement and success rates (p.53);
*   qualification overall and timely success rates (p.56);
*   qualification Minimum Levels of Performance (p.58);
*   lesson observation grades;
*   learner progression, such as value added (p.62);
*   learner attendance and punctuality;
*   learner and employer satisfaction;
*   the use of additional support activities and funding;
*   destinations and outcomes, such as employment;
*   Framework for Excellence performance indicators (p.72).

The data and/or targets can then be categorised by, for example:
*   funding model and type;
*   learner age, ethnicity and gender;
*   learning difficulties and/or disabilities;
*   learner home postcode and level of deprivation;
*   provider curriculum or management area;
*   provider type or locality;
*   qualification sector subject area, type, Level, length and prioritisation;
*   national and local benchmarks (p.101).

The volume and types of data, along with the number of ways to cut, slice and dice it can be very daunting. What remains critical is that each provider considers their own circumstances, and uses data to support their judgements and actions associated with raising attainment. This includes the setting of appropriate targets within action plans, often as part of the self-assessment report, and then monitoring their success or otherwise.

As part of the quality assurance the most improved colleges had set targets which were clear, measurable and attainable, yet challenging. There were clear links between the institutional targets set in the strategic plan and the targets set at all levels throughout the organisation, including those set in service areas. Monitoring progress against targets was systematic and rigorous and seen as the responsibility of all.

Source: *How colleges improve, a review of effective practice*, Ofsted (September 2008)

Improving self-assessment

Ofsted has expressed a concern that the quality self-assessment has in some areas declined. As the graph below shows, the number of colleges graded as Outstanding for the quality of their self-assessment actually fell from 32% in 2007/08 to 15% in 2008/09.

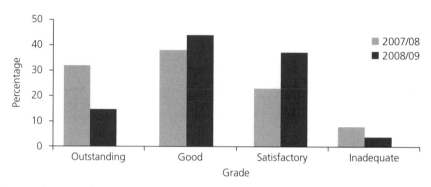

Source: *Talisman 80*, Ofsted (December 2009)

When Ofsted reviewed effective practice in colleges, the findings made clear that the use of data and targets within self-assessment was critical.

Key drivers for improvement	Barriers to change
Performance at all levels constantly monitored and analysed using accessible and reliable data	Poor data and data management
Ambitious yet realistic targets set on retention, attendance and pass rates	Lack of accountability; performance not managed because standards have not been set clearly
Well-informed governors who challenge managers vigorously on the college's performance	Insufficient challenge where there is poor performance; performance management either nonexistent or weak
One of the key findings from the review	
The better colleges had embedded a culture of accountability based on universally understood indicators of success. The systematic use of good, accessible and reliable data to analyse performance at all levels and identify areas for improvement was embedded throughout the organisation. All staff understood what the data told them and how they could be used to measure success.	
One of the key recommendations from the review	
Get the data right and make sure governors, managers and staff can interpret them.	

Source: *How colleges improve, a review of effective practice*, Ofsted (September 2008)

Beware the benchmark

National averages and the individual provider performance of qualifications are published. This means provision can be compared to a range of averages, known as benchmarks. This was a particularly popular approach before 2009, and Ofsted inspection reports included the provider success rates (for long provision by age and qualification type) alongside the relevant national averages. However, Ofsted have commented that they can be used inappropriately, and no longer include them in their reports.

The two examples below show, at the extreme, what should be avoided:

- The benchmark for a particular qualification is 50%, and a provider considers their provision to be good, simply because their success rate for the same qualification is above the benchmark, at just 55%.
- The benchmark for a particular qualification is 95%, and a provider considers their provision to be satisfactory, simply because their success rate is 90%. It is more likely this provision is outstanding.

National benchmarks

In most cases national (England) benchmarks are used to measure the performance of retention, achievement and success rates. In the statement below Ofsted advises caution:

> A common theme in the underperforming colleges visited which has an impact on students' success was the use of national averages to measure performance. Since their introduction, national benchmarks published by the Learning and Skills Council have been a useful tool, enabling colleges to measure their performance against other institutions in the sector. However, their use has too often, albeit inadvertently, reinforced the view that compliance with average performance is somehow a legitimate aspiration. A whole vocabulary of justification for satisfactory performance has built up around national averages.
>
> Source: *How colleges improve, a review of effective practice*, Ofsted (September 2008)

Local benchmarks

It is also possible to use benchmarks to compare, for example, success rates with similar providers in a locality. Commissioners will do this when tendering for provision, and providers might also include local benchmarks within their self-assessment report. However, again, as the Ofsted statement below shows, providers should be cautious of this approach.

> In a college originally judged good by inspection prior to the introduction of the Learning and Skills Council benchmarks, managers at all levels measured their performance against locally generated benchmarks, comparing similar colleges in similar localities, rather than national benchmarks. As a result, they considerably overestimated their own performance.
>
> Source: *How colleges improve, a review of effective practice*, Ofsted (September 2008)

Agencies and organisations

> Managing data quality is about embedding a culture of data excellence as part of the business. *The information authority* and Data Service have seen the need for such quality data and are taking positive steps to ensure providers are equipped with the information they need.
>
> Alys Reeves, Director of Finance, Start Training Ltd

The Data Service

The information authority

Managing information across partners

Other performance and data related organisations

This final chapter takes a closer look at the work of some of the post-16 education and training agencies and organisations listed below:

- Alliance of Sector Skills Councils
  www.sscalliance.org
- Association of Colleges
  www.aoc.co.uk
- Association of Learning Providers
  www.learningproviders.org.uk
- Department for Business, Innovation and Skills (p.110)
  www.bis.gov.uk
- Department for Children, Schools and Families (p.110)
  www.dcsf.gov.uk
- Department for Work and Pensions
  www.dwp.gov.uk
- England's Regional Development Agencies
  www.englandsrdas.com
- Higher Education Funding Council for England
  www.hefce.ac.uk
- Higher Education Statistics Agency
  www.hesa.ac.uk
- Joint Information Systems Committee (p.111)
  www.jisc.ac.uk
- Learning and Skills Improvement Service (p.111)
  www.lsis.org.uk
- Local Government Association
  www.lga.gov.uk
- Managing Information Across Partners (p.108)
  www.miap.gov.uk
- National Apprenticeship Service
  www.apprenticeships.org.uk
- Office of the Examinations and Qualifications Regulator
  www.ofqual.gov.uk
- Office for Standards in Education, Children's Services & Skills (p.111)
  www.ofsted.gov.uk
- Qualifications and Curriculum Development Agency
  www.qcda.gov.uk
- Quality Assurance Agency for Higher Education
  www.qaa.ac.uk
- The Data Service (p.104)
  www.thedataservice.org.uk
- The Information Authority (p.106)
  www.theia.org.uk
- UK Commission for Employment and Skills
  www.ukces.org.uk

The Data Service

The Data Service was launched in April 2008 to manage the collection, transformation and dissemination of all further education data. It is funded by the Department for Business, Innovation and Skills and is located within the Skills Funding Agency.

The Data Service key strategic aims and priorities:
- identify the scope of FE data and transition appropriate products into the Data Service;
- establish a long-term funding mechanism for a sector-led Data Service;
- achieve a 'Single Version of the Truth', identifying where multiple versions of the truth exist in FE and eliminating them;
- establish a single point of governance for each FE data set and their usage;
- develop a breadth and quality of services that react to market requirements whilst continuing to deliver excellence in existing services;
- work with and support *the information authority*.

The Data Service Steering Group:
- provides sector assurance on the development of the Data Service;
- represents the views of their community and is responsible for consulting with them on issues raised through the Group;
- provides feedback on the performance of the Data Service on behalf of their communities;
- makes proposals and recommendations on Data Service products and services on behalf of the communities they represent;
- supports the Data Service in engaging with their communities directly;
- reaches agreement with the Data Service programme on a framework of principles for Data Service operations;
- adjusts the Data Service scope to reflect sector interests and priorities.

The Data Service are responsible for:
- the Learner Information Suite software (*p.42*);
- the Learning Aims Database (*p.32*);
- the online data collections system (*p.28*);
- the Provider Gateway (*p.15*).
- publishing Statistical First Releases (*p.18*);
- publishing success rate and benchmark reports (*p.52*);
- publishing data quality reports (*p.86*);
- maintaining a comprehensive data dictionary on their website;
- providing dedicated support for customers which includes account management; a central help desk; and training for providers.

"By 2011 we will have evolved into an independent organisation acting in the interest of the further education sector as a whole." (www.thedataservice.org.uk/about)

E-learning from the Data Service

In November 2009 the Data Service launched an e-learning tool about the individualised learning record (ILR), which is available from:
http://ilrelearning.thedataservice.org.uk

"This tool has been developed to support providers with their understanding of the ILR, to assist with staff development, to help train new staff on the ILR and to update providers/staff on the 2009/10 ILR changes."
(www.thedataservice.org.uk/News/e_learning.htm)

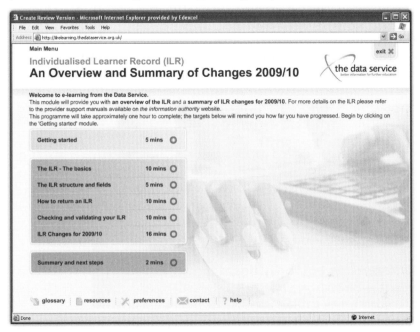

The e-learning tool also contains an extensive glossary of terms, as well as summarising some of the ILR changes for 2010/11 (p.30).

Cheylesmore House
Quinton Road
Coventry
CV1 2WT
T: 0870 2670001
E: servicedesk@thedataservice.org.uk
W: www.thedataservice.org.uk

The Service Desk is open Monday to Thursday 8.30am to 5pm and Friday 8.30am to 4pm and a range of e-mail alerts, such as for news and updates, can be subscribed to from the Data Service website.

The information authority

The information authority was launched in October 2006 to set and regulate data standards for all organisations involved in further education and training provision in England. This followed recommendations for such a role in The Foster Report (November 2005) and the subsequent White Paper: Further Education: Raising Skills, Improving Life Chances (March 2006). *The information authority* is funded by the Department for Business, Innovation and Skills and located within the Skills Funding Agency.

The information authority's strategic aims and priorities:
- improve data quality (*p.86*);
- continue to develop data standards with the Information Standards Board (ISB) for education, skills and children's services;
- address data burden and reduce bureaucracy (including representation on the Bureaucracy Reduction Group);
- continue to improve the Individualised Learner Record (ILR) specification and guidance;
- improve the ILR process and annual cycle;
- support the Data Service;
- engage with local authorities and new agencies, including the DCSF Star Chamber, which scrutinises data requests made to schools and local authority children's services;
- produce a learner data strategy.

The information authority board

Although *the information authority* is a shared service function within the Skills Funding Agency, it reports to a decision-making board with an independent chair. The board meets four times per year, is made up of 15 members that represent a range of further education related organisations.

The priority for *the information authority* board members is to ensure:
- the principles of *the information authority* are followed and that the use of data is maximised and burden is minimised;
- the wider interests of the FE system as a whole are supported – and not just the interests of their own organisations;
- representations from the system, through the secretariat, are considered so that data user and data provider stakeholders can influence board decisions;
- stability and appropriate notice of change to FE data standards.

Perhaps the most critical board meeting in 2009 was held on 2 December, when the members considered and ruled on 60 ILR change requests for 2010/11 (*p.30*). In many cases change requests were rejected, even those from Government departments. Board agendas, minutes and related documents are published on *the information authority* website. Find out more at http://tinyurl.com/yh3a4e9

The information authority online network

Upgraded and relaunched by *the information authority* secretariat in December 2009, feconnect is an the online network for those working with data in the further education and training system. In early January 2010 feconnect had 281 registered members contributing to a range of discussion groups. To find out more and contribute to discussion groups, or simply read what others are asking and replying, visit: http://forums.theia.org.uk/

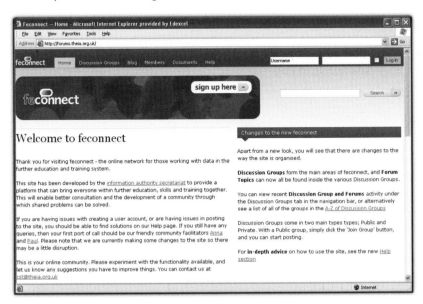

The information authority also runs advisory group meetings throughout the year to encourage system-wide participation and collaboration to improve the sector information systems and avoid, identify and resolve information and data issues. Find out more at http://tinyurl.com/d4zpop

the informat❶on authority

setting data standards
for further education

Cheylesmore House
Quinton Road
Coventry
CV1 2WT
T: 024 7682 5658
E: cst@theia.org.uk
W: www.theia.org.uk

The information authority has an online community and discussion group at http://forums.theia.org.uk and an e-newsletter which is subscribed to by emailing informnewsletter@theia.org.uk. *The information authority* is on Twitter at: www.twitter.com/theia

Managing Information Across Partners

In 2002 the MIAP Programme was established and is funded and strategically led by the Department for Business, Innovation and Skills. It is a UK-wide initiative designed to deliver a streamlined information management system for the education sector, supported by more than 40 partner organisations. MIAP is, in the main, responsible for three management information systems.

1. The Learner Registration Service (LRS)

The LRS generates a ten digit Unique Learner Number (ULN) for learners aged 14 and over, which acts as a single common identifier for UK learners. The ULN is then recorded by the provider into the Individualised Learner Record (ILR) field number L45 (*p.26*).

Learners will retain the same ULN for accessing their Personal Learning Record (*p.109*) throughout their lives, whatever their level of learning and wherever they choose to participate. When Precious Igbinobaro enrolled on a BTEC National Diploma in Health and Care at Lewisham College in September 2006 she was the first person to be registered with a ULN. By the end of 2009 more than three million ULNs had been allocated. There is an LRS Helpline (0845 602 2589) and further information at: www.miap.gov.uk/products/lrs/

Once logged in to the LRS users will be presented with the screen below.

2. The Personal Learning Record Service (PLRS)

The PLRS brings together information in one place already collected by education bodies (including demographic details, learning particpation and achievement) providing a lifelong record which learners can share with education providers and employers if they choose to do so. The PLRS pilot began in September 2008, and consisted of 22 providers and 84 learners.

The Personal Learning Record Service Invitation

MIAP

The Personal Learning Record Service is now "being released under controlled conditions" and at the time of writing MIAP were inviting organisations to adopt the new service. "If your organisation would like to lead the way, and be one of the first to use the Personal Learning Record Service, please email your contact details to lrssupport@miap.gov.uk. A team member will then be in touch to discuss how we progress together. A full induction briefing will follow and comprehensive support will be provided as you adopt the service." (MIAP Newsletter, December 2009)

3. The UK Register of Learning Providers (UKRLP)

The UKRLP allocates an eight digit UK Provider Reference Number (UKPRN) to act as a single common identifier for UK learner registration bodies, as well as brokering key information about learning providers to enable data sharing. There are more than 20,000 providers in the UKRLP, although it does not quality assure nor accredit the learning provision of the provider. There is a UKRLP Helpline (0845 202 1600) as well as a dedicated website: www.ukrlp.co.uk

Note

It is important that providers use the UKRLP website to check that their contact details and any web addresses are up to date and correct.

MIAP
Managing Information
Across Partners

Cheylesmore House
Quinton Road
Coventry
CV1 2WT
T: 0845 602 2589
E: lrssupport@miap.gov.uk
W: www.miap.gov.uk

In addition to publications on their website, MIAP has an e-newsletter which is subscribed to by emailing newsletter@miap.gov.uk

Other performance and data related organisations

department for children, schools and families

DCSF is the Government department which, amongst other things, is responsible for the policy and funding of 16–18 learner-responsive and Apprenticeships under the age of 19.

Department for Children,
Schools and Families
Sanctuary Buildings
Great Smith Street
London, SW1P 3BT
T: 0870 000 2288
W: www.dcsf.gov.uk

DCSF publishes a monthly *14–19 Delivery E-newsletter* subscribed to from their website. DCSF can also be followed on Twitter (www.twitter.com/dcsfgovuk), YouTube (www.youtube.com/dcsfgovuk) and Flickr (www.flickr.com/photos/dcsfgovuk)

BIS | Department for Business Innovation & Skills

BIS is the Government department which, amongst other things, is responsible for the policy and funding of adult learner-responsive, 19+ Apprenticeships and Train to Gain.

1 Victoria Street
Westminster
London, SW1H 0ET
T: 020 7215 5555
W: www.bis.gov.uk

BIS publishes a monthly *FE and Skills E-newsletter* which is subscribed to from their website. BIS can also be followed on Twitter (www.twitter.com/bisgovuk), YouTube (www.youtube.com/bisgovuk) and Flickr (www.flickr.com/photos/bisgovuk)

YOUNG PEOPLE'S LEARNING AGENCY

SKILLS FUNDING AGENCY

Young People's Learning Agency (YPLA) and the Skills Funding Agency replaced the Learning and Skills Council (LSC) on April 1 2010.

Cheylesmore House
Quinton Road
Coventry, CV1 2WT

Ofsted is the Office for Standards in Education, Children's Services and Skills. It regulate and inspect education and skills for learners of all ages (*p.94*).

Royal Exchange Buildings
St Ann's Square
Manchester, M2 7LA
T: 08456 404045
E: enquiries@ofsted.gov.uk
W: www.ofsted.gov.uk

Ofsted also produces a newspaper called *talisman*, for employees and learners in the learning and skills sector, 10 times per year. Subscribe at: http://live.ofsted.gov.uk/talisman/

The Learning and Skills Improvement Service (LSIS) is the sector-owned, governed and monitored improvement body. LSIS provides a wide range of services and works with the sector to develop practice.

Friars House
Manor House Drive
Coventry, CV1 2TE
T: 024 7662 7900
E: enquiries@lsis.org.uk
W: www.lsis.org.uk

LSIS publishes regular policy updates and a monthly e-newsletter which can be subscribed to from their website. LSIS also administer the www.excellencegateway.org.uk website which is rich with resources and support materials for learning and skills practitioners.

The Joint Information Systems Committee is an independent advisory body that works with further and higher education to support the use of technology in learning, teaching, research and administration.

JISC

Brettenham House
5 Lancaster Place
London, WC2E 7EN
T: 020 3006 6099
E: info@jisc.ac.uk
W: www.jisc.ac.uk

JISC provides many popular email forums, including one for college staff to discuss and share information about management information systems, performance statistics and analysis, funding and student data returns. Visit http://tinyurl.com/yfxdzud

Performance and data calendar

This calendar includes the ILR return dates for both learner and employer-responsive provision (*p.29*). You may wish to add other deadlines, such as internal report to the senior management team or the governing body.

April 2010						
MON	TUES	WED	THU	FRI	SAT	SUN
			1	2 Bank holiday	3	4
5 Bank holiday	6	7	8 09/10 W08 deadline	9	10	11
12	13	14	15	16	17	18
19	20	21	22	23	24	25
26	27	28	29	30		

May 2010

MON	TUES	WED	THU	FRI	SAT	SUN
					1	2
3 Bank holiday	4	5	6	7 09/10 W09 deadline	8	9
10	11	12	13	14	15	16
17 09/10 F03 deadline	18	18	20	21	22	23
24	25	26	27	28	29	30
31 Bank holiday						

			June 2010			
MON	TUES	WED	THU	FRI	SAT	SUN
	1	2	3	4 09/10 W10 deadline	5	6
7	8	9	10	11	12	13
14	15	16	17	18	19	20
21	22	23	24	25	26	27
28	29	30				

July 2010						
MON	TUES	WED	THU	FRI	SAT	SUN
			1	2	3	4
5	6 09/10 W11 deadline	7	8	9	10	11
12	13	14	15	16	17	18
19	20	21	22	23	24	25
26	27	28	29	30	31	

_____

_____

_____

_____

_____

_____

_____

_____

_____

_____

			August 2010			
MON	TUES	WED	THU	FRI	SAT	SUN
						1
2	3	4	5 09/10 W12 deadline	6	7	8
9	10	11	12	13	14	15
16	17	18	19	20	21	22
23	24	25	26	27	28	29
30 Bank holiday	31					

_____

_____

_____

_____

_____

_____

_____

_____

September 2010						
MON	TUES	WED	THU	FRI	SAT	SUN
		1	2	3	4	5
6 09/10 F04 deadline 10/11 ER01 deadline	7	8	9	10	11	12
13	14	15	16	17	18	19
20	21	22	23	24	25	26
27	28	29	30			

_____

_____

_____

_____

_____

_____

_____

_____

_____

_____

October 2010

MON	TUES	WED	THU	FRI	SAT	SUN
				1	2	3
4	5	6 10/11 ER02 deadline	7	8	9	10
11	12	13	14	15	16	17
18	19	20	21	22	23	24
25	26	27	28	29	30	31

_____

_____

_____

_____

_____

_____

_____

_____

_____

November 2010						
MON	TUES	WED	THU	FRI	SAT	SUN
1	2	3	4 10/11 ER03 deadline	5	6	7
8	9	10	11	12 09/10 W13 deadline	13	14
15	16	17	18	19	20	21
22 09/10 F05 deadline	23	24	25	26	27	28
29	30					

_____

_____

_____

_____

_____

_____

_____

_____

_____

_____

December 2010						
MON	TUES	WED	THU	FRI	SAT	SUN
		1	2	3	4	5
6 10/11 LR01 deadline 10/11 ER04 deadline	7	8	9	10	11	12
13	14	15	16	17	18	19
20	21	22	23	24	25	26
27 Bank holiday	28 Bank holiday	29	30	31		

_____

_____

_____

_____

_____

_____

_____

_____

_____

January 2011

MON	TUES	WED	THU	FRI	SAT	SUN
					1	2
3 Bank holiday	4	5	6	7 10/11 ER05 deadline	8	9
10	11	12	13	14	15	16
17	18	18	20	21	22	23
24	25	26	27	28	29	30
31						

_____

_____

_____

_____

_____

_____

_____

_____

February 2011						
MON	TUES	WED	THU	FRI	SAT	SUN
	1	2	3	4 10/11 ER06 deadline	5	6
7	8	9	10	11	12	13
14 10/11 LR02 deadline	15	16	17	18	19	20
21	22	23	24	25	26	27
28						

March 2011						
MON	TUES	WED	THU	FRI	SAT	SUN
	1	2	3	4 10/11 ER07 deadline	5	6
7	8	9	10	11	12	13
14	15	16	17	18	19	20
21	22	23	24	25	26	27
28	29	30	31			

April 2011						
MON	TUES	WED	THU	FRI	SAT	SUN
				1	2	3
4	5	6 10/11 ER08 deadline	7	8	9	10
11	12	13	14	15	16	17
18	19	20	21	22 Bank holiday	23	24
25 Bank holiday	26	27	28	29	30	

May 2011

MON	TUES	WED	THU	FRI	SAT	SUN
						1
2 Bank holiday	3	4	5	6 10/11 ER09 deadline	7	8
9	10	11	12	13	14	15
16 10/11 LR03 deadline	17	18	19	20	21	22
23	24	25	26	27	28	29
30 Bank holiday	31					

June 2011						
MON	TUES	WED	THU	FRI	SAT	SUN
		1	2	3	4	5
6 10/11 ER10 deadline	7	8	9	10	11	12
13	14	15	16	17	18	19
20	21	22	23	24	25	26
27	28	29	30			

July 2011						
MON	TUES	WED	THU	FRI	SAT	SUN
				1	2	3
4	5	6 10/11 ER11 deadline	7	8	9	10
11	12	13	14	15	16	17
18	19	20	21	22	23	24
25	26	27	28	29	30	31

_____

_____

_____

_____

_____

_____

_____

_____

_____

_____

Notes

HAVERING COLLEGE OF F & H E

138877

WITHDRAWN